The Soma People

Lopa Mukherjee

ISBN-13: 978-1505351347
ISBN-10: 1505351340

First published in 2015
Lopa Mukherjee, 1973- **author**
      The Soma People / Lopa Mukherjee. pages ; cm
      Novel
      ISBN 13: 9781505351347
      1. Spirituality--Yoga. 2. Spiritual Powers.
      3. Self-help. 4. Fiction, Indic (English). I. Title.

Disclaimer: This is a work of fiction. Names, characters,
places and incidents are either author's own imagination or
are used fictitiously. Any resemblance to real persons, living
or dead, or actual events or locales, or organizations is
purely coincidental.

Preface

He who wants to find his higher Self must begin the journey of the inner world. It can be a hard endeavor given the many dazzling distractions of the outer world, but for the indomitable spirit there is more adventure here than in the discovery of the ten thousand things.

In this story a novice finds a group of spiritual seekers. Their masters command powers commonly termed as *supernatural.* But once the spiritual transformation begins these become as natural as thinking. These powers are described in the story without using their yogic terms. Their Sanskrit names are listed here for those who want to link them to yogic achievements, called siddhis: prakamya, vyapti, aishwarya, vashita, ishita, mahima, laghima, trikala drishti, parakaya pravesha.

The masters invite the novice into their world and guide him step by step, until he faces an adventure so exciting he becomes a child again. Every day he learns something new. Starting from material science and using the rational method they lure him beyond the mind's boundaries. He begins to see hidden truths and *perceive* what he merely *saw* before.

But not all who live around the masters are as capable as them. They have to battle against their weaknesses – anger, delusion, greed… and battle each other's lower nature. But whoever said the discovery of the Self would be a dull excursion? The adversaries may be strong, but the Guidance is stronger.

So welcome pilgrim-warrior, to the adventure of consciousness.

Contents

Prologue

Mr Henderson was a well-known name in the pharmaceutical industry. He grew his firm from pharmacy to factory and was the envy of his competitors. Everybody knew him to be a jovial man who could afford his sense of humor. His standard joke was "And then I will go to India". People thought he meant, "After this deal, I will take a vacation." Only his son, Paul, knew the truth.

When Paul was still in middle school, his father had a setback. A prominent distributor sued him for fraud. His Soma pill did not induce the calm it claimed to induce. Mr Henderson lost the case and would have to suffer a considerable loss, but for his cunning. He passed on the loss to his supplier. This man was Mohan Das, seller of herbal medicines in India. The magic ingredient of the Soma pill was shilajit, obtained from the Himalayas. It is a mineral substance that oozes out of rocks. Collecting it is a dangerous task. One has to scale the mountains above the tree line, swing from rope ladders to reach the rocks, and scrape out the precious organic mud. Only during the short summer months is this undertaking possible.

Shilajit is rare and expensive. When Mr Henderson told Mohan Das his last batch would not be reimbursed because the drug was ineffective, he knew he was treading on moral quicksand. And so he came across as an angry customer. It is not that his business would have folded, but his hundred employees, and himself most of all, would suffer a year or more of no raises and no bonus. He had to

1

worry about the mortgage on his mansion, his wife's lavish parties, his son's college fees. He had no idea how it would affect Mohan Das. A fleeting thought made him wonder about the man – did he have a large family, did he own a house, was someone sick in his household? But it was best not to find out. He could not afford it at this point in time.

So a few months later when he held the letter postmarked "India", he scowled. He would not negotiate. It was hard enough to save his reputation. The letter from Mohan Das read:

Dear Mr Henderson,
I must thank you for changing my life. What I initially saw as a setback has turned out to be a blessing. Wishing you peace.
Yours faithfully,
Mohan Das

The pharmaceutical giant was intrigued. Had Mohan Das answered some big questions of life, such as how to be happy? He read and re-read the letter and puzzled over it. Then decided he had to talk to Mohan Das. It was not so much guilt, but curiosity that drove his quest.

When he contacted Mohan Das's office he was told the pharmaceutical company had folded. There was no forwarding address. He then realized the magnitude of his action. Yet why did the man not punish him, at least with bitter words? Was he sending him a message in that letter?

To know it if he had to meet Mahan Das personally, he would do it.

For years he planned to visit India, a place he had feared for tropical diseases and lack of law and order. He began reading about the country and found he had been terribly ignorant about it. For example, he did not know how shilajit was collected, that only certain villagers living in the barren tundra had the skill. Did they also get affected by the setback? Did Mohan Das pass on his loss to them? What did Mohan Das do after he was chased out of his business?

But the trip always got postponed, and one day it was too late. A stroke confined Mr Henderson to the wheelchair. Then he spent all his effort goading his son to take the trip on his behalf, to find Mohan Das and ask him all those questions. He watched Paul getting sucked into the company. He watched him fall in love. He watched him cut down on sleep and rest. He watched his son as a flashback of himself and feared that one day he too would undercut somebody. He too would suffer guilt that would corrode his being. He too would live the rest of his life feeling something crucial was missing. But Paul never found the time for the trip and one day it was too late.

Mr Henderson's will came as a shock. He had given instructions to sell his company and distribute the money to charities. There was a clause though that Paul hung on to. He would inherit everything if he could visit India and find out from Mohan Das why he had thanked his father when

3

he was being bankrupted. There was a sum marked out for Mohan Das and his former employees. Within a year this task had to be accomplished for Paul to own his father's legacy.

Chapter One

India

Paul leaned against the parapet and surveyed the scene in front of him. The morning mist was rising. Gradually green patches of grass floated up to his vision. A woodpecker knocked against a tree trunk. A bird called. Another replied. There were tall trees from where their voices swooped down. He heard the buzzing of bees. How loud they sounded in the quiet morning!

Then suddenly his eyes stopped short in their casual flitting. He saw limbs and bodies moving rapidly. In the middle of the lawn a man stood surrounded by eight men. Each had a wooden pole he was thrusting at the man in the center, who was blocking them with his own pole. The poles were of a man's height an inch thick. Paul realized there was no woodpecker. The pecking sound came from the poles striking each other. From the loudness of the impact he guessed the poles were of some strong wood, bamboo most likely. One vertical blow on the head could crack it open. The man in the center whirled around, plunged to let a blow go past and at the same time tackled another. The buzzing came from their poles chopping the air. Paul ran downstairs and stood on the veranda facing the group.

He observed each man's movement and found he had a style of his own and a rhythm of his own. The man in the center was a coiled spring, who seemed to know a split second before where the next blow would come from.

Chapter 1

Once his block was vertical; the next second it was horizontal. At times he rotated his pole so fast it created a wall that threw back any attacking pole. Sometimes he twisted his pole and flung the opponent's pole into the air. The man's movements were so graceful he seems to be performing a dance. Only in films had Paul seen such stunts, and he knew those were filmed with many cuts in between. His body stiffened as the blows rained down and he made flinching movements to avoid them. His nerves raced. He had begun to perspire in anticipation of the blow that would break the central figure. It was a question of time; the body can last only so long.

And so it happened. The sparring ended. But not as Paul had feared. The man in the center jammed his pole on the ground, yanked himself up vertically, feet leading the way, like a pole-vaulter. He flew over the heads of his opponents and landed behind them. Before they could turn around and surround him, he had sprinted out of sight. He was a one of God's finest works - in looks, in strength, in skill.

Paul started to clap. The eight men turned around and looked at him. Soon they were all clapping. Then their gaze fell beside Paul and they stopped abruptly. Paul followed their gaze and found he was staring at one of Michelangelo's paintings that he had seen on the ceiling of the Sistine Chapel.

"Good Morning," said the apparition. He had a long white beard and equally long hair, both cascading down his handsome torso. A white shawl was flung across his chest. His legs were covered in a dhoti. He held himself like a king, upright and confident. His eyes smiled and so did his mouth. The early morning sunlight gave his face a luster as of a full moon. Paul was taken in by his charisma.

"Good Morning," he replied, "Are you the father?"
"I am a brother, like everybody else here."
"I mean, you are the leader of the ashram. Aren't you?"
"If we measured leadership by length of beard I may have been. But we have no leaders here. My name is Satyananda."
"I am Paul Henderson. Nice to meet you."
"Don't be so sure," laughed Paul's new acquaintance, "So Mr Henderson, how did you come here?"
"You can call me Paul."
"People here call me Satyen."

So how had he come here? Paul thought about the journey to Arunpur and smiled. He had to board a train from the city. Through its glass panes Paul saw the countryside passing by in page after page of serene beauty. He wanted to get out and stand in the middle of a banana grove, by a small pond with water lilies covering half the surface. Women had come to wash clothes and utensils in one side. Men were getting ready to bathe, oiling themselves and doing squats on the pool's edge. His co-passengers chatted with him freely and participated in his wonder. The city had choked him to despair. The milling crowds, the chaotic traffic, the polluted air, the relentless noise. And above all, people staring at him, urchins pulling at his sleeves and extending their palms. It was all too shattering an experience. The bell boy peering into his room. The waiter looking around searchingly. Paul's smile vanished. Then he thought of the last leg of the journey, and the smile returned.

There was no taxi he could hire, so he had to catch the bus. It bumped along with a belly-full of people and Paul expected a breakdown at any moment. But it did not come and the people made space for his oversized backpack. Again the large black eyes were fixed on him. This time when he made eye contact, he smiled. No more "Hi"s. And the people smiled back. He was thrilled. He had solved a big problem. He turned in every direction, looked into people's faces and smiled. They smiled back. It almost became a game. Very soon people looked his way and offered their smile before he could. The mirth was catching on. When some of them got down, they waved him goodbye. No words were needed. Gestures spoke eloquently.

He piled his backpack on a rickshaw and got out his camera. The scenes of the town floated past him. The smile never left his face. Some of the strangers on the road smiled back. One said, "Welcome". Another wished him, "Good morning" and he responded with the same enthusiasm, although it was evening. And finally he reached the stately archway of the ashram. The gate opened before he could knock. A young man gestured him in and stepped aside for the rickshaw. He said, "Welcome, Mr Henderson. We have been expecting you."

But surely Satyen did not want to know the details of his journey. Did he want to know how he was sent here? The story about Mohan Das? Or how Paul used a private investigator to reach Mohan Das's son? And how the kind son wrote to the ashram where his father was living? Paul mused for a while before replying. He was facing a wise man who would not be interested in mundane talk perhaps. So carefully crafting his answer he said, "I have come here to look for the soma people."

Satyen was pleased with the answer. Smiling broadly he replied, "In that case, I may be able to help you."

Paul had done some homework and had found Soma was not just the name of a pill but had a meaning in the Indian language. It was a magic potion the Gods drank. Surely Mohan Das had found a way to produce this special beverage. Maybe some of the herbs the ashram grew were for soma. Perhaps there was a chance of reviving the Soma back at home. Not as a pill but as a drink. He could not wait to ask. "Very kind of you. So may I ask, have you found some way of making this magic soma potion?"

"Aha, you want to get to the soma already? But have you seen the gods who drink this soma? Maybe when you see its effect on them, you will know better what to do with it."

Paul hesitated, "I am not, you see, a very religious person. I mean, I skipped going to church all my life, except when it was a museum of sorts."

"It's alright, we are not religious either. Yes, we have a room full of deities, but there is no ceremony between us and them. As for rituals we are completely ignorant of them. This is our meditation hall and is open to all, any time of day or night. Every evening you will see people from the town gathering here for a silent meditation."

Satyen entered a room. It was so dark Paul could see nothing inside. But as Satyen opened the windows Paul saw a strange vision unfold before his eyes. On a platform at the far end of the room was a magnificent array of statues. Some of them were life sized, and some smaller. Some had many arms and they sat on swan and tiger and peacock and rat. The women seemed to be the warring sort. Especially frightening was a black one with red tongue hanging out, spear raised to strike. As he stared at her he thought she was naked. Her body was covered by a garland made of big spheres like painted coconut shells. Then he strained his eyes and imagined he saw a man's head. As his eyes traveled round the garland he was convinced he was seeing heads. Each was severed at the neck and had a bloody edge. These hapless heads were strung together by their hair.

"Formidable, isn't she?"
Paul winced. Satyen was observing him.
"Yes," he whispered, "And that one too with the many hands. And this one with an elephant's head. Who are these creatures?"
"They are gods and goddesses."
"I beg your pardon. I thought the gods were supposed to be hidden from sight, in dark chambers. I was told it was symbolic of the womb. That is why the sanctum sanctorum

in temples is a small dark room." Paul was quite proud of his information gathering skills.

Satyen replied, "Then perhaps the gods were born by the time they reached here."

Paul suspected Satyen was playing with him. But Satyen provided an explanation, "At least they don't mind revealing themselves to us. And revealing too their true nature! Half of them are at war, the other half involved in taming wild animals, - if they are not themselves half animal - and a few are engrossed in playing musical instruments. Fine keepers of humans, you say?"

Now Paul had to voice his concern, "Surely you are joking with me?"

"No, I am joking with the gods."

"I suppose you can afford to blaspheme, being a monk and all that."

"Blaspheme? There is no such concept here. I wish you had said 'being a friend of the gods and all that…'"

"Well, then introduce your friends to me."

Satyen pointed at each statue and let fall a few kind words for each of them. Some of them were known for their exploits and these too he related. Paul listened in rapt attention. Only when the last deity was passed did he realize there were people in the chamber. Some were seated with eyes closed; some followed Satyen and listened to his stories. Incense was lit and the room was filling up with its perfume. Satyen pointed at the altar and said, "If you want to light incense the sticks are in that box. There are some earthen lamps in that niche. You can light them too. Many like to meditate in the dark, but if that lady scares you, light as many lamps as you like."

"To be frank, yes, she does. She is so …"
"Monstrous?" Satyen was laughing now, and others around him smiled at Paul. "I will let you on a secret," he continued, "Her task is to kill demons and every time she goes to battle, do you know what gives her the strength to fight?"
"What?"
"Soma. Because these demons are really tough. And who do you think are these demons? They are in us. The ugly thoughts, moods, desires, habits we carry within us. So beware and don't you expose your defects to her. If you want to pamper yourself, that is. If you want to get purified, then by all means meet her head on. And what more, you are really lucky to be so close to her here."

Paul asked with as much calm as he could muster, "You are speaking metaphorically, I presume?"
"Oh no," replied Satyen, "I am not merely playing with figures of speech. You have entered a world of symbols. Are you ready for it? How much time do we have to beat about the bush anyway? Not much. There are so many things we need to do in life, of which so much adds up to nothing, isn't it? Of course you could begin to question them. I believe you are ready. You have yourself led me to bring you here. Aren't you looking for soma, that symbolic magic potion? And you spoke about the womb-like sanctum which is symbolic temple architecture. Now you have met the symbolic gods and their symbolic battles. All

you have to do now is create a language from these symbols."

Chapter Two

Soma

Paul and Satyen came out of the meditation hall. Immediately Satyen was encircled by a group of people who were waiting to see him. A young man came forward and beckoned to Paul to follow him. He showed Paul the dining hall and the sink and told him about the meal timings. He turned to leave but Paul called him back, "I am looking for Mr Mohan Das. Do you know him?" The man answered, "The doctor? Yes, of course. The whole town knows him. You will find him around here soon." So Mohan Das was a doctor too? Did his father know it?

Paul served himself some breakfast and sat at a table. The others nodded and smiled, and continued eating in silence. Paul felt relaxed and happy. He had not felt this way ever since he had landed in India. Nobody was staring at him. He wasn't inadvertently hurting sentiments. They did not pass any judgment on his appearance or his conduct. He was being accepted. He loved the tropical fruits he was eating and the milk was so tasty! He liked the coarse bread and the music of metal spoons striking metal bowls.

He thought to himself how much at ease he felt in the ashram. In fact he had not felt so content in a very long time. The last time was when he was watching a sunset from the top of a hill. They were all watching the sunset – his father, mother, uncle, aunt, cousin, the cat. They had all hiked up the hill with their picnic baskets. He had carried the cat up in her own little basket. After a lazy meal they had watched the sun sliding down the horizon. It was as quiet as here. But that was a long time back. When he was ten years old; during a vacation. He looked around at the faces and all he saw was serenity.

As Paul was coming out of the dining hall he heard from behind, "Good morning, Mr Henderson." Paul turned to find a man his father's age. Instantly he colored, overcome by his father's guilt. But Mohan Das was much too amiable a person to hold grudges. He stepped back and stared at Paul approvingly, "I had always imagined your father to be like this – handsome, trim, energetic. How is he doing?"

The two went to Mohan Das's consulting chamber and talked. Mohan Das was sorry to hear about the elder Henderson's passing. He was interested to know about the pharmaceutical firm, much to Paul's embarrassment. The older man asked detailed questions on medicine composition, how they were positioned in the market, who their competitors were. At no point was there any bitterness for what was done to him. Finally Paul came to the crucial part of his story - about his father's dearest wish to visit Mohan Das.

"Why me?" asked the older man.

"Oh, I forgot to refresh your memory. Give me a minute, let me run up to my room and get something."

Mohan Das read his letter and smiled, "So the letter had an impact? Your father was my professional partner and as you perhaps know the last part of our relationship wasn't simple. This is a personal letter. I wrote it after I came here. I had found the *silver bullet*, as Americans say. But this is how *I* would say it – I found the true soma. Are you following me? Not the pill, the true soma. And I was pushed to discover it with your father's help. So I thought I owed him something. There was a chance he would take it seriously and consider something more than material wellbeing. What I hear from you really pleases me. But I am sorry that he was broken-spirited for years! Why did he not do anything about it?"

"He wanted to learn your secret; very badly, in fact, but could not extricate himself. And then he wanted to send me, and I too kept delaying it, until it was too late."

"So you have come to learn my secret?"

Just then some patients knocked on the door and the doctor got busy. Paul came outside the chamber and to his great delight saw that the pole combatants were back on the lawn. The men were sparring in pairs. The hero of the morning was their instructor. Paul's hands were itching to hold a pole and learn some moves. The hero beckoned to him and he came scampering like a child. The instructor pointed to a shed, "You will find poles there." Paul actually uttered a wild "Yeah!" and then came to his senses. The other men's faces were wreathed in crescent moon smiles.

The instructor showed him some elementary steps and told him he would spar with a partner after he mastered these. Paul practiced diligently. Once or twice the instructor passed by and corrected his moves. Suddenly he looked up and saw Mohan Das standing outside his chamber smiling at him. Paul waved back excitedly, "I have been recruited!" He had forgotten that their conversation had been interrupted and he had a secret to learn from him.

The highlight of the day was when the hero casually stuck his pole in Paul's way and almost made him trip. Paul regained his balance and struck back at him. Something told him this was a test and this insolence was actually welcome. And so it was. He had been promoted. He would spar with an opponent. And who else but the formidable instructor himself! After many appreciatory comments from the instructor Paul felt at ease to start a conversation.

He asked, "Is this martial art for defense or offence?"
"Neither," came the reply, "It is to gain self-mastery. Once you have it you can use it for anything - defense or offence. But we have a problem to start with. Can you tell me what it is?"
Paul shook his head. The keen eyes of the man made him feel empty-headed. And it was a gorgeous feeling. Not the emptiness of ignorance but the emptiness of freedom from preconceived notions. He was ready to learn everything from the beginning again. The man said, "The problem is that we have no clue what the *self* of the *self-mastery* is."
"Right, so what do we do?" asked Paul puzzled.
"We begin the journey of the discovery of the self."

He went away to inspect the others. Paul practiced his moves. His empty mind gave his body a lot of room and his moves resembled steps in a dance. Once he looked up and caught the eye of the instructor, who nodded in approval. Paul felt as elated as a child would after impressing his parents.

He was so tired he fell asleep after lunch. Late in the afternoon he rushed down to the clinic and found Mohan Das with a patient. He waited outside the chamber. He wasn't good at waiting. He jiggled his legs, then played making shadows with his fingers and soon ran out of creativity. What he wanted to do was practice the lessons he had learnt. He walked to the shed, found a pole and started practicing his moves. One of the brothers who was passing by corrected a move. Finally when it was getting dark Mohan Das emerged from his room. Paul returned the pole and came up to him.

Mohan Das remarked, "Looks like Indian martial arts has ensnared you. Or is it Hiren's magnetism?"
"Hiren? Is that the name of the instructor?"
"Hirendra, to be precise, but Hiren to be practical."
A tiny alarm bell started ringing in Paul's head. What if Mohan Das told him his secret? Then he would have no excuse to remain here. And what of the things he was learning? He wanted to apply the principles of torque the instructor had demonstrated. All he could say was a hesitant, "You must be tired after the long day of work."
The doctor smiled, "I see, *you* are in no mood to talk. Maybe you want to practice some more?"
"No, no, not at all," stammered Paul. "I was concerned about you. If you want to talk, let's do it."

The two ambled around the lawn and Mohan Das told his story, "I had always had an inclination to help people. As a child I was running around festivals putting up canopies and washing dishes. As a youth I participated in several teaching camps. During holidays from school I used to do odd jobs in the dispensary, tying bandages and measuring out medicine. I loved to heal people. My family was poor. I could not dream of going to medical college. I got into the business of selling medicines. But I wanted my son to become a doctor. That was when I was still blind. It took a financial crisis to open my eyes.

I was left without a job and no money to pass on to my family. It is then that my early self caught on with me. Did I not want to heal people? So what was I doing with my life? My son was old enough to take care of his mother. And without the money for his medical college he could study languages and become a teacher. That is what he genuinely wanted to be. Not a doctor. That was my dream I was imposing on him. So you see it turned out well for him too.

For a few months I roamed around India looking for a community where I could volunteer. The idea was that they would take care of my livelihood and I would contribute with my labor, that is, as a naturopath. There would be no other monetary transaction. I found this place, came here as a visitor, but have never left. There are a lot of people here who need healing. They like my cures. I had enough chance to fulfil my material needs in my professional life. And yet there was this huge need within I could not tackle. I was feeding my body and starving my soul. Satyen summarized it well, 'Soma was staring you in the face all those years and finally when push came to shove you understood its meaning'."

"Tell me more about soma. I only knew it as a brand name, but here I learnt it was the nectar of the gods." "Very interesting how a word full of meaning becomes a trademarked product and loses all its original potency. I am thinking of the word *yoga* also. Sad how it is reduced to a set of postures. Yoga is the union of the soul with its Source. And its journey has so many routes, traverses so many levels of consciousness, with so many intermediary destinations…it is impossible to explain it in a few words. Anyway, let me tell you about soma. You are right, in our wisdom texts they speak about a certain drink that energizes the gods. These gods then get as though on steroids and perform miraculous tasks, such as killing demons of monstrous shapes, creating parallel universes, composing hymns. When humans drink soma they too are filled with great possibilities."

"Have you drunk it?" "Unfortunately the formula of the drink was never very precise. It does mention certain plants; a rare genus of lotus in one case; some have surmised it is a psychedelic mushroom. But to answer your question, soma is not a mainstream drink. Maybe some people make it. There are lots of secret practices in spiritual groups. But firstly, is it even a drink?" "*You* said you found the soma here?"

"I found what the adepts wanted *out* of the soma. That is the real finding. And that is the secret your father wanted to learn."

Paul was silent for a while, thinking it over. Then he said, "It is not easily conveyed, is it?"

"It cannot be conveyed, my child. It has to be experienced."

"How much time does it take?"

Mohan Das laughed aloud, "That too cannot be conveyed. Stay some more."

"May I?"

"Of course."

Paul's heart leaped. He had become a child again. Then he remembered the other important task, "I almost forgot. Wait here while I run to my room."

He handed over the money, "That was the amount my father owed you."

"I told you, I need nothing," Mohan Das tried to hand him back the packet.

Paul lifted his hands, "Use it for a cause. Besides I too have everything I need." Paul felt a glow of pride saying it. Then he realized with a shock why. It was because he had never said it before. Paul with his estate and cars and friends and factory had never articulated this simple fact.

Mohan Das accepted the packet, "In that case my patients will not need to buy medicines for a long time. I thank you and your father for your generosity and I hope your father's soul will rest in peace."

Chapter 2

Paul had not written back home or to his company manager. Nor to his lady love. But they would have to wait. The dinner bell was going and after that there was the incense-filled mediation hall.

Chapter Three

The fairground

Paul sat up. It was no use trying to sleep. Every time he dozed off he found himself kissing the brown face of the woman. She tasted like chocolate. But as soon as he nestled close to her neck, he woke up. He was sweating and the night was airless. She was the pickle vendor at the fairgrounds. He had spent the better part of the day standing at her stall. She had beckoned to him as he stood photographing the jars of pickles. She dipped her spoon in one of the jars and extended the sample towards him. He gestured towards his stomach and shook his fingers rapidly. She laughed and reached out for another jar. "No no," he said. "Meetha, meetha [sweet]," she replied. Her voice was sweet and her lips meeting and parting threw him off balance. Like a child he copied her, "Meetha" and received the glob she poured in his hand.

It was sweet but sour too and he jumped up and down as his salivary glands protested. She laughed and he scrambled for the camera, as though she was an exotic bird he had to capture on film and this moment would not return. She was laughing again. He had smeared the camera with pickle jelly. She wiped it with a towel, "Bechara, tcha, tcha [poor fellow]," and her voice sounded like a flute. The rest of the day slipped past instantly. He stood at her counter and they conversed understanding none of the words they spoke. When people came to buy pickles she introduced him and she exchanged pleasantries with them.

He laughed along. He had her on film, her every gesture, even some words he had learnt from her.

Paul walked out of his room and went downstairs to the meditation hall. Here there were many things to distract him - the statues grouped in their extended families with a menagerie of animals at their feet. He saw a figure in the room, sitting still, back erect. He decided to take a walk outside. The figure spoke. He recognized the voice to be Satyen's.

"No sleep tonight?"

"No, very hot. Maybe I will have a drink."

"Will water cool that kind of heat?"

Paul wondered what he meant by that.

Satyen got up and accompanied Paul outside the room. They walked out of the ashram. The heat wasn't oppressive any more. Paul relaxed. "Do you know where the pickle vendor lives?"

"There are several pickle vendors here."

"Twenty something, pretty girl."

"The whole place is infested with that sort."

"Let's go to the fairgrounds. I will show you the stall."

"Here we are," said Satyen and spread his arms wide. It was an empty space with no stalls.

Paul shook his head, "This isn't the place."

"Yes, it is, don't you recognize the banyan tree?"

Paul noticed it and cried out in disbelief, "It's all gone! Was this the last day?"

"No, tomorrow morning they will return. Now they are all dead in their beds."

"Dead? I think not. Take me to that girl and I will show you how alive people can be."

Satyen laughed, "And then what? Another day of chitchat and another night of fantasy?"

"So you saw me talking to her? Find her for me and you will see how fantasies can become realities."

"I will, tomorrow night."

"OK," Paul swallowed hard, "OK, tomorrow."

"Some nights are very potent. They can extinguish everything. All the fretting and sweating and expecting."

The next day Paul raced to the pickle vendor's stall. A man was in her place and he sneered at Paul. He said something that made passersby laugh. Paul walked away. She must be there in the crowd somewhere. Surely she wanted to meet him as urgently as he did. He would find her. He walked in derelict circles enticed by the cries of vendors, bumping into people jostling past him. The sun was beating down mercilessly. He would have to return to the ashram to refill his water bottle. Near the cooler he met Satyen.

"She is not there!" he exclaimed, despite himself.

Satyen replied, "Come with me."

They walked through the fairgrounds and reached the other side of town. They kept walking towards the hill. They climbed the hill and turned around. Down below the festivities unraveled themselves in kaleidoscopic gyrations. There was a distant hum and tiny moving colors. "Good view," said Paul and rested his water bottle on the ground. They sat in silence. He scanned the grounds looking for her. It was a ridiculous exercise. He could not see any face clearly. His eyes chased the red spots. That was the color of the sari she had worn yesterday. Satyen was sucking on a blade of grass and leaning on one elbow.

"Why did you bring me here? asked Paul, irritated.
"To see."
"See what? I have no binoculars. The camera's zoom lens is too weak."
"Try this," Satyen extended a fresh blade of grass.
Paul sucked at it, "Yuk, is it neem or something?"
Satyen smiled lazily, "Bitter even now?"
"Of course. As hell. No wait, I think it has an aftertaste. Sweet maybe? Yes, sweet, almost nice."
Paul relaxed on one elbow like Satyen as he sucked at the stem. His eyes fell on the fairground. He sat up abruptly. "I see her!" he yelled.

She was at her stall, cupping one cheek in her palm. Women were around her, begging her to show the cheek, consoling her, swearing at her husband. Even through her tears she was counting the money and doling out portions deftly. He saw her face and recoiled. One cheek was swollen grotesquely. How? He asked in shock. And he provided the answer too. Her husband had slapped her. Why? Because she had been flirting with the white man. She was weeping but happy beneath her tears. Business was brisk. People came to stare at her face, heard her complaints, sympathized with her, and left only after having bought something from her.

But she was happy for another reason too. She knew she had made her husband jealous. So he did care for her after all! He lied when he said he cared more for his cows because they had cost him more. If they strayed he never beat them so hard. Tonight he would make up. Already her body trembled at the thought.

Paul turned his gaze away. The thing in his mouth tasted bitter again. His eyes fell upon a group of boys playing kabaddi. One of the boys was under a whole pile of boys. He was screaming in pain. The boys were making so much noise they could not hear him. When they let him go they found his leg was twisted from the knee. They hauled him onto a tractor. It was a slow vehicle but faster than the bullock cart. One boy cycled ahead to warn the doctor.

The hospital was five miles away. He whimpered for a mile and then fainted. Blood oozed from the splintered knee. He would reach too late and they would amputate the limb. He would walk in crutches all his life. Find no wife, no employment. Start drinking and gambling. Get involved with some gangsters and be roughed up. Die in his brother's toolshed coughing up blood. "No!" gasped Paul. He would reach the hospital on time and they would fix his knee. He would be a farm hand, have a good wife and two children. He would die in his own house, made of cement and bricks, at eighty years of age, surrounded by grandchildren.

A balloon burst loudly. It had belonged to a little girl. Some boys were teasing her and had pierced her prized possession. She started crying. Her mother could not hear her. She was trying out necklaces at a stall a few paces away. She was not really keen on the necklace. She wondered what her husband was up to in the city. She suspected him. Her father-in-law lay sick at home and was not dying. She was tired of the unsophisticated townsfolk. Someone gave the little girl a bite of cotton candy. She was laughing again, balloon forgotten.

Sand had blown into the eye of a young woman. A lad nearby was blowing air into it. His fingertips were groping her exposed midriff and the other hand was sliding down the shoulder. She squirmed in his grasp but was also bringing herself closer to him. If their parents saw them together they would be beaten. He was a carpenter and she was a teacher's daughter. They would run away after three years of secret courtship - just as far as the train took them for five rupees. They would room in a cheap hotel and return announcing she was with child. The families would consider them dead. The newlyweds would move to the next town. He would make furniture and she would sell pickles during festivals. She would flirt with customers and have her photos taken by them. At night man and wife would dream their separate dreams.

Paul pulled his head out as though it was stuck into a telescope. The colors of the fairground became a jumble. Each one was a speck, indistinguishable from the other. He looked up at the sun and down again at the human drama.

All he could see were movements blurring into a white haze. He pressed his eyes with the balls of his palms.

"What is it?" asked Satyen.

"Sunstroke," he mumbled and fell upon his back.

After a while when he regained his balance, he turned towards the reclining figure beside him, "Say Satyen, is it possible that I saw those people down there?"

"If you did I should say it was a prescient sunstroke."

"Not only did I see them, I also knew why they were doing what they were doing. Not only that. I knew what was going on in the head of one of the ladies. Also I saw a young unmarried couple whose life would eventually become like the pickle vendor and her husband's."

"Maybe you saw a flashback of how they met. Or maybe all the meetings are alike, all the developments are alike, all the endings are alike. A twist here and there to mark the difference. In essence there is but one story repeated innumerable times. All these separate colors blend into one white mist."

"Yes, that is what I saw too at the end. They were all disappearing into a haze."

Paul closed his eyes. The white mist was rapidly vanishing too. All he was seeing was the blackness of night. It was an empty ground, no stalls, no movements, no plans, no desires. Only was left a prescient silence.

Paul sat up again, "I saw a boy who broke his leg and I saw two totally opposite outcomes from it. This accident was the turning point of his life. And everything depended on how fast he could reach the hospital."

"You saw the possibilities his destiny could take. What it *does* take is another matter. It knows what is best for the boy's evolution and it will do accordingly."

"Will he lose his leg and live a wretched life henceforth?"

"Wretched in whose eyes? Yours? His own? Society's? Eyes without knowledge are as good as blind. What do these blind eyes mean to the Prescient one? Nothing at all. Our guiding hand does not turn away from pain. It uses everything as a means. Only the outer being is shaken, the inner person remains calm. You flinch from pain because you are identified with the wrong person."

"How can I become the inner person?"

"Witness the human drama. Witness yourself in the human drama. Witness the planetary drama, the universal drama, the drama unfolding in space and time. Witness what could be, what ought to be, what should *not* be. Witness what was, what is, what will be. Witness everything and be not shaken. Do not cast your vote either way. Remain the impartial balance. And in that poise you will begin to *see*. Your new sight will lead you to your inner being."

Chapter Four

Bird

The children scrambled up the tree after the bird. Just as they were an arm's length away the bird hopped on to a higher branch. The little pursuers continued their ascent. The boy on the highest branch stretched out his hand. But the bird flew away; not very far, to another tree within the compound. The children ran down their tree and started climbing the new tree. Here too the bird hopped about a few times. Then she flew low over the grass. The boys followed, sprinting after her. She flew in circles. Some of the boys reversed the direction of their chase and hoped to meet her head on. But she saw through their trick and flew up. She was perched on the first floor balcony. They made for the stairs, panting and sweating. When they reached the balcony, the bird flew to a bush below.

Paul noticed Hiren was standing on the veranda facing the garden. He was looking at the bird intently. As the children reached the bush Hiren moved his head and the bird seemed to follow his movement. He rested his eyes on the sandpit and the bird came to rest there. The children dived in the sand, but Hiren's eyes had risen up in the air. He held his gaze steady and the bird made tiny circles over the sandpit. The children were getting tired and some of them did not get up from the cool sand. One or two staggered out and chased the bird, which had perched on a branch again. But they fell on the grass and lay there panting. Hiren walked out in the open and the bird came to perch on his shoulder.

The children surrounded him. He said, "Today also you have made the same mistake. You all know that the bird is swifter than you. You have an advantage though, and that is what you need to find. I will give you a hint. *Each* of you is trying to be the bird catcher. Why did I say it is a *team* game? Think about it and next week we will repeat this exercise."

The children dispersed. Paul accosted Hiren, "That's an impressive toy you have. Where do you hide the remote control?"

"In here," Hiren pointed to his head.

"Oh sure!" laughed Paul, "Can I try my hand at it?" he reached out to touch the bird. It flew away uttering a squeak. Paul blinked in surprise, "Now, I must say, it's a fine piece of work. I almost thought it was a real bird."

"It is real."

"Your pet? You tamed it pretty well."

"I did not tame it; it's wild."

"Then why didn't it fly away? You must have clipped its feathers."

"Look there!" Hiren pointed. The bird had been sitting on a window sill. Just as Hiren pointed, it flapped upwards and when it was above the outer walls, it flew away.

Paul had not expected to find hi-tech electronic devices in an ashram. But he was ready to revise this impression. He requested Hiren to show his secret. Hiren was happy to be searched. No microchip was found hidden on his person, or in his hair. His fingertips were normal flesh and blood. He had no pockets, wore no sandals. Paul threw up his hands incredulously.

In answer Hiren started a discourse on migratory birds: how their precise return to the same nesting grounds was a mystery for decades. And how science had some answers now. "They have found that birds produce electromagnetic waves. This field interacts with the earth's electromagnetic field which enables the bird to navigate. And how do we know this? We have been able to attach magnets on the bird and have seen them go astray. Since the earth's field is constant how do different species have different routes? Because this is passed on down the generations. Once a fledgling makes the first journey it creates an electromagnetic map that it stores in its memory. And how do we know it? We have captured birds that have never made the journey and seen they are incapable of making it. As a last discovery scientists have even found a gland in the bird's brain that could be the source of the electromagnetic waves. All creatures have this gland, at least those that came after the bird in the evolutionary chain. And since every bird has this gland they can all produce electromagnetic waves, whether they are a migratory species or not. All one has to do to control a bird's navigation system is to influence that electromagnetic field."

Paul had been searching Hiren and had found no source of electromagnetic waves; not even a rudimentary valve radio. And then Hiren went on to explain something which made Paul stumble backwards.

"If a bird's small brain can produce waves why not of a more evolved specie's? Such as man? If a man modulated his electromagnetic field in the right way he could persuade the bird to go places. Simple, isn't it?"

"My God, are you saying you made a bird fly at your own will? You know where this could lead to? I mean as a tool in men's hands? If you can control a bird, next you can control another beast, say a tiger, or an elephant…"

"Or another man?"

"My God, I had not thought of it. Why are you smiling?"

"I am happy to see an adult who has not lost his sense of wonder."

"But listen, Hiren, you cannot implant thoughts in others and make them act your way. That will be a breach of people's fundamental rights."

"Why don't you penalize advertising agencies? They are always suggesting. Many people are even acting on those suggestions. Every person who expresses himself is guilty in some way. Others are hearing him or reading his writings and forming opinions. Punish your teachers and your parents for giving you new ideas. In fact punish yourself first. Your past is stored in your subconscious. It floats up as thoughts and alters your free choice. And what is worse the subconscious is working all the time – recording every sensory experience, even those you are unconscious of. Later these are regurgitated as thoughts and ideas, inspirations and desires, habits and phobias. Punish your senses. They are constantly informing your mind and triggering thoughts. Punish your mind. It is poaching on the environment all around.

There is hardly a person who can create a new thought. Yes, we are always altering thoughts we get and disguising them in our own colors. We delude ourselves thinking them to be our own creations. But trace their source and you will know how little we are original creators of thought. No, really, do this exercise. For a few minutes jot down every thought you have. Then find their origin. Remember what you were hearing, seeing, smelling; ask people around what they were thinking, find out what the TV was showing, dig in your past. You will be surprised how little freedom of thought you have. If you are ready to let these unknown sources pass, why not allow a source you trust? Surely you trust me?"

Paul remonstrated, "But nobody would believe one man can directly control another."
"That is good news. It is hardly a toy humans – underserving humans – ought to have access to. Mankind does not have a good track record in handling power."
"But don't you want the deserving humans to know about it?"
"You can tell them if you want to. I am not interested in convincing people. It took many lives and a noble death to tell humans the earth wasn't the center of the universe."
"But that was because they did not experience it themselves. They relied on their senses those days."

"Not senses all the time. They trusted their elders, the priests, the wise men of their age. Now too it is the same. You trust some scientists and think it is a great leap forward? Every age has created its own boundary of knowledge. You have done the same. The ideas that fall inside you term scientific and acceptable. The ideas outside are unscientific and impossible. This boundary has expanded over time. Once to cure we bled a person, now we give him blood. We call this progress. Now we accept the subconscious as real. We treat it to cure us of psychological problems. We trust doctors to inject us with chemicals. We allow them to cut us open."

"We trust only after many successes. We trust the numbers."

"Yes, that's right. If Columbus's entire crew did not swear they saw new land, the Spanish king would probably not believe Columbus. If enough people said there was a super-conscious, just as there is a subconscious, would you believe it?"

"Yes, then I would."

"But enough people *are* saying it. Yogis and psychics and mediums and occultists *are* saying it. In addition they are saying the super-conscious has many solutions to our problems. Will you still resist it? The frontiers of knowledge have been expanding over time. Our human story is not over, so why should it not go on expanding? Open the windows of your mind. Let in some light."

Paul suddenly felt empty headed, a liberating empty headedness; not a baffling one. He had experienced this before. Yes, it had been during the pole exercise. He looked around at everything as if they were suffused with a new essence: the trees, the crows pecking at the leftovers, the boy washing the vessels, Hiren at his side.

Suddenly Paul knew the boy washing the vessels would get up. The next moment the boy shut off the tap and got up. Then Paul knew he would go to the flower bed. The boy walked to the flower bed. Paul knew he would shake his wet hands over the flowers. The boy shook his hands and sprinkled water on the flowers. Paul knew a bee would fly out of a flower. A second later he saw the bee. It rose in the air. Paul knew it would come his way. The bee flew in his direction. Paul knew the insect meant no harm. It thought Paul's hand had pollen on it. The bee landed on his palm; tickled it. Paul felt a deep love for this tiny creature. He wished there was pollen in his hand. Paul knew the bee would fly away and return to the flowers. Immediately the bee rose and flew straight to the flowers.

Paul wondered what was happening to him. He heard a voice answer him, "Just as an electric current creates an electromagnetic field, a thought creates a thought field. Stronger the thought the stronger is its influence. A thought field can plant thoughts in a receiver. And who is a receiver? Another mind - mind of man, mind of a bee. We do it all the time to our own minds. We call it will-power, or positive thinking. Even fear and despondency we plant within ourselves with the power of negative thoughts."
Paul asked the voice, "So these events that just happened, was someone planting these thoughts in the boy's mind, in the bee's mind?"
"Yes."

"How did I know beforehand what would happen?"

"Because the same person planted those thoughts in your mind a split second earlier."

"It is you, Hiren, isn't it? And you controlled the bird with your thoughts. Not with your electromagnetic field?"

"There are many ways to achieve the same result. For example I can speak with you, or I can transmit the words in your mind without using the medium of sound."

"Then why did you tell me about the electromagnetic field?"

"Because it is one of the many possibilities. But most importantly because you wanted a scientific explanation. This was the only way I could invite you here. Now that you experience will you believe?"

Paul nodded.

The voice went on, "Usually our will-power is diffused, like white light. But one can train it to be concentrated. Diffuse light will then become laser light."

Paul looked sideways at Hiren. Hiren smiled. They were both seated on the steps of the veranda facing the lawn. The boy had finished washing, the crows had gone, the flower bed was still. Paul held Hiren's hand for an instant and squeezed it. He wanted to say "Thank you", but words felt too gross for the moment.

Chapter Five

Fate

Paul had been going round in circles for a while. The town was more complicated than he had imagined. The shops and houses he had used as landmarks kept returning. Then he heard the voice of succor. Someone was speaking in his language! A lady called out from the window of a house. "Excuse me, is there any way I can help you? I have been watching you pass this spot a few times."

Paul replied eagerly, "Yes, just what I need! Do you know where the ashram is?"

"Yes, definitely. I can tell you. Just a moment."

She opened the door, "Please come in. I have seen you at the ashram once. Can I make you some tea?"

And that is how Paul made his first connection with the townsfolk. She taught the Bhagavad Gita, and her students called her Madhu-di. Later he would spend afternoons in non-trivial conversations with her and sometimes eavesdrop on her class. But on the first encounter they were quite formal. The only personal touch was when he pointed at a photograph on her writing table and asked, "Who is that young man there?"

"Raja, my son."

"What does he do?"

"He is no more," answered the mother. After that, conversation was difficult and very soon Paul got up. Madhu-di gave him a book she had borrowed from the ashram and asked him to return it.

Paul handed the book to Satyen, who remarked, "So you have met Madhu?"

"Most conveniently, I would say. I needed direction, she needed a messenger."

"Is that all you see? Just a coincidence?"

"Why, do you see anything more?"

"You both are tied by another bond. She lost a son, you a father."

"Oh, but we could not speak of our grief. In fact, she does not know of my loss."

"When you say *know* you mean by the mind. But the mind is an imperfect instrument. It can be bettered, and that is why we do mental exercises. Do we *know* why things happen to us? Perhaps you think they happen randomly. No, there was a purpose why you met Madhu. And why she met you. You may never find out, but that does not mean there was no purpose."

"If a hypothesis cannot be proved, then it is as good as wrong."

"Right or wrong you do not know. So maybe you can leave it at *irrelevant*? Let me tell you a story."

"A householder had a wife who complained about everything. He was not the ambitious kind, was happy with his middle-class job and mediocre lifestyle. But she wanted to see profit every year and acquire bigger and better things. As you can imagine there was little peace. During one of his trips here he met me and disclosed everything. And then a year later I heard him loud and clear in my head. His call came to me; he did not come in person. I went to the city where he lived. Went to the police station and found him in the lockup. This is what had happened:

Husband and wife had gone to Darjeeling on vacation. When walking on a steep hill the wife slipped and fell off the cliff. Her family heard of the death and accused him of murder. It was no secret that the couple was unhappy. He had no witness to exonerate himself. But I *knew* what had happened. He had wanted freedom from his domestic troubles and fate had listened to his prayer. The man was too weak to give up his wife, so fate had to take the harder path. I explained it to him. He understood. We both *knew* it was a question of time when his fate would come to his aid again. All I had to do was to convey the message to the wife's family. I told them I *knew* he was innocent."

"And they believed you!"

"No, they shooed me away. They believed in the court of justice set up by man. But the court of justice set up by karmic laws is much more powerful. Within a year he came to see me. He had been set free by the same people who had wanted him dead. People in his wife's family had started falling sick and losing money. They asked an astrologer to help them. He advised them to withdraw the case. All of a sudden all their misfortunes vanished. I told you this story to give you an example of a higher knowledge. We all have access to it, but like a muscle this higher mind needs to be trained."

It wasn't the knowledge aspect of the story but the death that disturbed Paul. He asked, "Are you saying death is always deliverance?"

"No, death is not an easy topic. Many scriptures have devoted entire passages trying to explain it."

"Can you give me an idea of what they say?"

"If there is one event in life that alters a person most, it is the death of a dear one. Let me tell you another story. Once there was a rich and happy family - father, mother and son. Son grew up, studied management and got a good job. Parents' lives revolved around the son and his work and his wedding and his friends and his travels. It could have gone on thus for another thirty years until the parents died of old age. The son in his time would repeat the same story.

But fate willed it otherwise. The son was in a bus that met with an accident. Many people in that bus died, but not all. The son was one of the dead. Suddenly someone had pulled the carpet from under the parents' feet and knocked them off. Friends' sympathies did not console them. They sold the house in the city and gave up all their old connections. They moved to a small town and started taking stock. It is then that I met them. They wanted to find out why this had happened to their son. Did he commit any misdemeanor? Why had it happened to *them*? Did *they* commit any misdemeanor? Or was some evil eye upon them? And now, what should they do with their lives?

They had to start from the beginning. Whatever you learn in books remains in books until you experience them. The true language of knowledge is not Latin or Greek or Sanskrit or Pali. It is the language of experience. To understand death you have to understand Life too."

"Did they understand then why he had died?" asked Paul surprised.

"They understood with an understanding that is not mental understanding. It is a knowledge that a higher mind can access. They began training their mind and were graced with the understanding."

Suddenly Paul connected the dots, "Are you talking about Madhu-di?"

"Yes, her son's *death* has given her *life* a new meaning."

"And her husband?"

"He passed away last year. He had aged gracefully like her and when he was departing they were both ready. There is One eternal which is not born nor does it die, but houses itself in creatures that are born and die. Let us call this eternal thing the soul. The soul gathers experience in a lifetime, then moves on to other lifetimes and gathers experiences from there. One who has the *knowledge* sees his own births strung together as we see days alternating with night. When he looks upon the death of another he sees that person's soul journeying from one day to another through the corridor of night. His soul suffers not when his heart grieves."

"But how do you explain an untimely death?"

"Untimely? What do we know of the soul's mission? When its task is done it goes. *We* call it accident. Often the person himself does not know his soul has decided to move on. After death he continues on his journey wearing a new set of clothes. The body, heart, mind, life-circumstances are nothing but a set of clothes…" And Satyen started quoting from the Gita, verse after verse of such beauty that Paul's eyes were washed in tears. He also understood why he had to meet Madhu-di. He had to hear this from Satyen, he had to learn the Gita from her, he had to understand his father's death.

Chapter Six

Cave

In the meditation hall Paul felt a tug on his sleeve. He looked up into the anxious face of a young man. He was about to speak when Paul gestured him to keep silent and meet him outside the hall. The two stepped out. The man introduced himself as Kavi. He needed help for some heavy lifting.

"Sure, no problem," said Paul and followed him.

On the way Paul tried to make light conversation but Kavi seemed preoccupied. Every question he asked had to be repeated, which was becoming rather tiring. When the row of houses thinned and the metal road disappeared into a cycle path, Paul asked, "Where do you live?"

"Near the Bharati Paper Mill. I work as an accountant there."

Paul stopped short. "We are going the other way… or are we not going to your place?"

"No. You don't mind, do you?"

"Not yet," murmured Paul, but added, "Where *are* we going?"

"Not far, just round the corner."

"There is no corner in sight," laughed Paul. He had been given such spurious directions before. People loved to plant their imaginary milestones "just round the corner", although the actual destination would be far away, or sometimes unknown to them. He caught himself thinking the last thought and stopped, "Wait, where are we going? How far are we from the place?"

Kavi walked on ahead as though he had not heard Paul. Paul trailed along, feeling uncomfortable. "Look, it will get dark soon and I need to meet someone this evening. Unless I know how long this will take I cannot go any further."

As a reply Kavi asked, "Do you have matches?"

"I have a lighter. Why?"

"Then we should be fine in the dark. I have a candle."

"Look here, I am not going on a wild goose chase with a stranger."

"Stranger? You have seen me so many times in the ashram. We have even stood side by side listening to Hiren and once you picked up my wallet that had fallen from my pocket."

Paul felt frustrated. So many people looked alike, at least to his untrained eyes.

Kavi walked ahead not looking back at Paul lest he call off the plan. The dirt path ended. The trees crowded in. A few minutes into the woods and Paul decided he would turn back. Just then Kavi stopped, "Here is the entrance." He produced a candle and a matchbox. "I have just a few sticks left but inside the cave there is no wind, so we should be fine. And if something happens, we have your lighter."

"Wait a minute," remonstrated Paul. "This is an unpleasant surprise. God knows what reptile is crawling in there or whose den we are trespassing."

"Don't be afraid. This is a cave I know from a long time back. I, we, I, we…long time back, or was it a long time back? We, I , we, I used to… oh, I know this place like the lines on my palm, then the lines went wild, and I, we, I, we…"

"You are making no sense, man!" cried Paul even more appalled to be sequestered with a madman.

Kavi looked stunned by Paul's anger. "There is nothing wild inside the cave. I used to keep my secret things in here. A tree started boring its roots inside it and has created a wall. I tried to pull it out but it is too strong. Maybe you can do it."

"Did you try using a saw?"

"Oh no! We have to do it gently. What if the tree fell down and the cave collapsed?"

"How big is the tree?"

"It did not occur to me… to find the offending tree, that is."

"You could chop the tree and then the roots may just fall off. We don't have to get into that hole."

"No, but we must!"

"Why? You said you were afraid of the tree falling down."

"But the cave has granite walls."

"Very well, then you are not afraid of the cave collapsing?"

The man looked puzzled. Paul asked again, quite sure his question was not heard, "Are you or are you not afraid of the cave collapsing?"

"One has to do what one has to do," was the reply, "Come."

Kavi walked in and Paul followed shaking his head in incomprehension. They entered the entrails of the earth and a foul smell hit them. Paul was choking. Kavi observed absentmindedly, "Must be the time of monsoons... Breathe normally, you will get used to the smell. It's alright usually."

"Where is that blasted root?"

Paul had decided to tug at it once or twice then declare they needed a saw and run out.

Then he almost stumbled on the crouching figure of Kavi.

"What the hell are you doing, man?"

"Nothing, nothing," came a mumbled reply but Kavi's hands were busy clearing away objects from their path.

"Look, I am not interested in your treasure. I just want to reach that godforsaken root."

"Treasure is beyond the root's wall. These are just... impediments."

Paul's curiosity was tickled. Surreptitiously he bent down and groped into the corner where Kavi had hidden something. He felt something soft. Picking it up and bringing it close to his eyes he saw it was a blouse. It had a glow of its own. He had seen such handiwork before. It was called zari, gold embroidered cloth, worn in special occasions, such as weddings. He groped some more and this time the flow of the drapery his hand touched told him it was a sari. For a second he lit his lighter and stole a glance. Yes, it was a richly embroidered sari of red silk with zari flower motifs all over.

"What was that?" Kavi whipped around.

"Fireflies," replied Paul and walked on, a smile hovering on his lips.

They came upon the root, but Paul was in a playful mood. He asked, "What do you have on the other side?"

"Never mind, trifles for a rich man like you."

"Just curious."

"Give me a hand."

"Not unless you tell me what you have hidden out there."

"I already told you!" Kavi sounded furious. His efforts at moving the root was obviously yielding no result.

"Wasn't satisfactory," Paul smirked in the dark.

"Can't a man have secrets?"

"Well, what do I get out of this? At least let me know. I won't blurt it out."

"Jewels. Silver and such."

"Gold embroidered sari but *silver* jewelry?"

Kavi's was silent for a while. Then he said, "They are my wife's – so don't you go thinking wrong things. Now will you please help?"

"Why are your wife's wedding garments here? Is the marriage a secret too?"

Kavi sat down leaning against the granite wall of the cave. Paul waited. In the dark he could see the root, or the tangle of roots. It was a mess out there. Many trees were above, or perhaps the whole forest was boring down on this one hole to peep into someone's dark secrets.

Kavi's voice came out choked, "I used to love her so much. We came here to … know each other when we were in the first blush of love. Then came the big wedding and everything started going downhill. She will not let me give anything to my sister, or mother or anybody else. But I have to buy things for her family. She hates them - my people. And calls them such names it makes me shudder. I never knew a woman could have such a foul mouth. Will not even spare *me* the abuses. I work like a dog for her, and do you know what she calls me?"

"What?"

"Dog!"

A big chuckle welled up into Paul's bosom which he suppressed with difficulty.

Kavi continued, "Nothing I do or say can make her happy."

"You could give up *your* family. That should keep her happy, no?"

"Never, why should I? I know them longer than I know her. And they have been good to me. Besides they are good to her too."

"Is she jealous?"

"Possessive. I am extra good to her now since I know she must be insecure. But it's of no use, no use, no use at all. If she has nothing to complain about she will rummage through the past and pull something out."

"Give her an ultimatum to mend her ways."

"I have pleaded a million times. Women… tears and drama."

"Ultimatum means something else. It does not mean pardoning when the tears flow or applauding when the drama ends."

"What are you suggesting?"

"Walk away."

"From her?"

"Yes, man, haven't you heard of divorce?"

"But what will the families say?"

"Hang on, let me get this straight. Isn't it your life? Or a collective family life?"

"You Westerners don't understand the many equations that are involved. What will she do?"

"Why would you care? It would probably force her to change her ways."

Kavi shook his head, "I could not do that! I promised to make her happy. I cannot fail. Give me a hand, will you, please?"

Paul pulled at the roots in as many directions as he could in that cramped place. This was no task for bare hands. He turned to conversation instead, "Do you think these treasures will help you in any way?"

"There are some she has not seen. I was saving them up for a grand occasion. I suppose that occasion has come, although it can hardly be called grand. But it's no time to regret the past. If this turns her heart I should feel grateful."

Suddenly Paul wanted a whip, not a saw. A whip to whip this slave of a man cringing before something so low. The tangle of roots budged not a bit. He cried, "What you need is a saw at the least. A dynamite would be preferable."

"No!" shrieked Kavi, "It would destroy the jewels. You Westerners won't get it. I was just wallowing in self-pity. My own fault - everything. I forced her to marry me. Now of course I cannot desert her."

"Oh, what a sacrifice!" remarked Paul.

"Are you being sarcastic?"

"Maybe..." chuckled Paul.

"Yes, mock us our family values. Let's go."

"Come back with a saw next time."

"Yes, thank you, and I hope you can keep secrets. Dynamite indeed!" he spat out vehemently. "What an absurd idea. It will destroy everything! All my painstaking labor for such a long time."

"Yes, man, mend, mend, but don't end," Paul laughed easing himself out of the hole.

"Can I admit defeat? Am I not a man?"

"Oh, so you think abandoning a rotten marriage is defeat?"

"We don't discard one toy and pick another just like that!"

"Even if the game is over?"

It was dark and they walked back in silence; one smiling, another sulking.

Paul asked Satyen if he knew Kavi. Satyen nodded. And did he know *about* Kavi? Satyen nodded again. Then without further hesitation Paul recounted the events of the previous day. Satyen smiled indulgently. At the end Paul added how difficult it was for him to understand this famed *promise*. How can a man gamble his life away for the sake of a promise? A promise he made anticipating something which did not materialize, namely, conjugal bliss! Wasn't he free to abandon the promise when its premise was defeated?

Satyen did not reply. He simply asked, "Where is that cave?"

"Let the cave be. I already let out most of the poor man's secret."

"And you want to keep your *promise?*" Satyen wore a stricken expression.

Paul smiled at the irony. He held Satyen by the elbow and dragged him along, "Alright, let's go, and wipe that mockery off your face."

They reached the outskirts of the village where the dirt road ended. Paul inspected the place but could not find the entrance to the cave. The trees looked familiar and there was even a granite shelf, but no cave. Satyen suggested they should climb the hill to get a better lay of the land. The climb did not help locate the cave, but it gave some clues. Paul noticed how small the trees were. They were also dry and almost brittle. It was a wild variety of eucalyptus, and its roots did not go deep. Some trees were leaning on one side, no doubt knocked by a storm.

With a saw on can clean up those roots easily. Paul felt satisfied that at least his advice to the poor soul was sound.

Suddenly Satyen whispered, "Shh." He had heard footsteps below. And sure enough the bush moved. Through the sparse branches they spied the figure of none other than Kavi. Paul nudged Satyen, "Let's follow him."

"The dry leaves will give us away," answered Satyen in a hushed tone.

"Then you wait and let me go alone. If he sees me I will say I came to look for the tree that could be above the cave."

"Wait. He is doing something."

They watched Kavi light the candle, duck down and enter somewhere. "We lost him now," whispered Paul, but the next instant he shook his head incredulously. Kavi was bent over and crawling along the trees as though he was inside a cave. There was no real cave. Both Paul and Satyen could clearly see his back. Often he stopped, picked up some dirt and clutching it close to his face rubbed it on his cheeks. The onlookers looked at each other and shrugged their shoulders. Kavi reached a tangle of roots that jutted out under the granite shelf. It was a small tree and the roots were exposed.

Kavi had no saw. He pulled at the roots weakly, then sat down leaning against the granite wall and started weeping in his hands.

"We must go to him," urged Paul, "Poor fellow."

Satyen shrugged. Paul called out, "Hey, my man. Look up."

Kavi rose to his feet but remained bent under an imaginary ceiling.

"Up here. It's Paul. You forgot your saw."

Kavi screwed his head up and knocked the candle over. "Ahh" he screamed, and began groping for it as though in the dark. He banged his head against the granite shelf and tripped on his own foot.

"What is he doing?" exclaimed Paul. "It is broad daylight and he needs a candle to walk? In a cave that's actually an open space?"

"Well, he is quite taken in by it; so much so he convinced you yesterday it was a cave."

Satyen and Paul climbed down the hill and did not care if Kavi heard them. He was no different than a bird or squirrel.

"Satyen, I say, what do you make of the man?"

"All I can say is don't fall into the trap of compassion. The advice is for you, not Kavi. Don't bother about him. He is doing what he likes to do."

"I disagree. He is trapped. Someone has to help him out. Like giving a poor man a loan. Otherwise how else will he pull himself out of the hole he is in?"

"Loan becomes alms when given to the wrong man."

"I still believe Kavi could do with some help."

"You have already tried. You asked him to get a saw. Did he get one? You tried to call him now and explain. You ended up frightening him."

Paul brooded for a while then spoke, "Surely you know about counseling. There are professionals who are specially trained to counsel on marriage problems."

Satyen replied, "We have that sort of thing too. We call them elders, trained in the school of life."

"Hah, one day Kavi will become an elder and will end up giving trashy counsel. Maybe he is at present getting trashy counsel from some *elder*, who's telling him it's some sort of defeat to fix your life. And victory if you suffer."

Satyen flashed an enigmatic smile, "Defeat or victory? Doesn't that depend on the battle you are fighting?"

They were walking past a grassy patch where a cow stood watching them mournfully. Her large brown eyes were swimming in tears and were so human-like that Paul stopped walking. Soon he found why she was in pain. She had twisted her rope round and round the tether and was tightly bound to it, unable even to bend down and chomp the grass.

"Poor thing, perhaps she does not know how she got into this mess."

Satyen grinned, "Are you planning to solve her problem too?"

"Satyen, this one's just a cow. She does not even have horns. All I have to do is lead her around the tether in the opposite direction. She will be one grateful cow today."

Paul walked towards her. The cow kept a close watch at the approaching figure. Her eyes turned from pain, to fear, to defiance. Only Satyen saw that. Paul was busy near her neck looking for a grip. Then in a split-second something happened to his buttocks. A frightful kick made him jump in the air. The cow was poised for a second kick. Paul leapt away clutching his bottom.

Satyen was laughing.

"It hurts!" yelled Paul.

Satyen laughed louder. Paul gestured a blow towards the irate cow and dusting his unfortunate posterior joined Satyen on the road.

Satyen remarked, "So sorry for you, you can't even help a cow!"

"I suppose," said Paul feeling sober. "No wait, I have an idea. The cow did not guess my intention. What I should have done is yanked up the tether and set her free. Let's go back!"

Satyen nodded wisely.

Paul turned around and froze. A woman was looking back at them from the patch of grass. As soon as she saw them turn she started hurling abuses at them, "You, son of a bitch, haramzada, behen chodh…" Paul could not catch many words but the few he did made him walk away faster.

"What a witch! Shouting like I milked her cow!" He gasped.

"Be a man, don't take it lying down," urged Satyen.

"Yeah, right!" Paul turned around and to his surprise he saw the cow, but no woman. The cow was stranded as before.

Paul stopped Satyen, "Did you see that! She must have flown away on her broom!"

"No," replied Satyen, "There she is."

Paul turned again. And there she was shaking her index finger at them. This time he looked past her and tried to spot the cow.

"Where is the cow, Satyen? Are they both bewitched? It was right there!"

"If you turn again you will see only the cow, and the next time only the woman, and then only the cow, and so on."

"You are joking, right?" Paul turned around, then looked in front, then again back, and front and back, many times. Satyen wasn't joking.

Satyen kept walking in his even pace, not once turning around. He said, "Now that you have met Kavi's wife, what do you think?"

"That was his wife? And what about the cow?"

"They are one and the same. She has pinned herself down and does not want any help. We create our own realities.

We live in them and get so used to them, we forget we had made them once and can unmake them any time. Kavi and his wife have enmeshed themselves in their own web. Other people's compassion has become their food, and unfortunately you were a fly they just supped on."

Chapter Seven

Work

The woman walked up to Paul and said, "Hello! See, I am real."

Paul had been staring at her as though he was seeing a ghost. She had the most outlandish ornaments on her. Paul wondered how the necklace did not choke her, why the clips on her head had to pinch her scalp, why the earrings made her earlobes look sore and red. But the worst thing was that this apparition was coming out of Hiren's room.

"Hello," he replied stiffly.

"Why are you looking at me that way?"

"I thought you came to see the doctor," he pointed at the doctor's chamber.

"Yes, so I did. But not the doctor of bodies; the doctor of souls."

"Oh, I did not know."

"Did not know what? That Hiren was a healer or that women have souls?"

It did not take long for the two to become friends. Paul shrugged his shoulders at the woman's getup. If these did not bother her, why should he be concerned? Two hours later Paul and Nisha were standing on a hillock overlooking the town. This was Nisha's workplace. Her colleagues were eager to show him how they squeezed venom out of snakes. The dried venom crystals were sold in the town's pharmacy. They also collected honey from the hives that hung from tall trees.

Chapter 7

Nisha was an activist-journalist who was helping the tribal people fight for justice. The hills were rich in minerals and were well forested. Some industrialists backed by the government wanted to wean the tribal away from their land and monetize their natural resources. They were felling trees and depleting the stock of fouls, which the tribal hunted for food. Nisha was there to educate them on the ways of the corrupt world, which promised to relocate them in a developed area, but in reality usurped their land and left them high and dry. She told them of other tribes that had trusted the corporates and now were working in factories and living in ghettos.

It wasn't easy fighting legal battles with money baskets. Being a woman further complicated matters. Unpleasant visitors approached her. But for some trusted allies amongst the tribal and some in the town, she would soon have given up. Her strongest ally was Hiren, of whom she spoke with immense devotion. Paul could see she yearned to live in the ashram, a safe haven full of peace, with ready access to mentors such as Hiren and Satyen.

She had asked if she could stay at the ashram's guest house. But the brothers thought she was too young and they would not be able to concentrate on their inner growth. "The same old problem. And penalize women for it!" she sighed. She asked Paul his daily routine and the way he interacted with the brothers and who cooked which day and what was taught in the classes. Some of the tribal people got carpentry lessons from ashram brothers. As for herself she went to the ashram when she needed help. The first brother she had met was Hiren and to him she had started confiding her problems. "He is a good listener and ever since he has become my mentor. If not for him I would have left this place a long time ago."

"What does he tell you?" asked Paul.
"Mostly about reward-less work. Offer your work to the divine and let Him decide the outcome. That is the only way to fight frustration. And to think of it, do we have everything in our control? At best we can try our best. Yes, of course we have to choose our battles wisely. Hiren has helped there too. It is amazing how much he knows about society, although he isn't part of society. I mean he is far away from ugly sentiments such as greed and egoism, but he knows exactly how much pressure to put on which man, what his weakness is, who should be pitted against whom. He is such a strategist! I wonder what he was before he came here. Do you know?"

Paul did not know. But he was intrigued about the concept of working without thinking about reward. Why work if you don't have the incentive of making profits? It would just not do in a corporate world. Tell your shareholders the forecast was in the hands of the divine?

Back in the ashram Paul asked Satyen about work. "The *what, why* and *how* of work are related. Start with answering *why* we work. Then answer *what* work we should do. Lastly *how* we should do it. Only then will you grasp why work is to be done without thinking about the results."

Paul rounded up all the people he knew. Kavi said whatever he did had one motive – to make others happy. It turned out these *others* were his wife, his parents, his sister, his boss. The rest did not count. Maybe it was true of most people. Didn't Paul's father do the same and wipe someone out of business to make his family comfortable? In Kavi's case he seemed to be doing poorly. Paul suggested maybe he should try pleasing the one person he could in fact keep happy – himself. Kavi retorted, "You think I would be happy living a selfish life?"

Paul asked Nisha who was then in an angry mood having just returned from the courthouse. "Why do I work? Does this look like fun to you? Living in a stinking hotel and getting abused by lawyers and capitalist marauders? You think I do it for my family? Do these people look like my blood relations? I do what I do because I believe in a cause. Justice and equal rights for every man."

Paul asked Madhu-di if she enjoyed teaching. "It can get boring and my voice hurts all the time. I do it to help the new generation. Someone did it for me when I was growing up. Now it's my turn to shoulder my social duty."

He asked some other men. Most answered they worked to give their kids a good livelihood. Many went a little further. "I earn to fetch my daughter a good husband. A good groom is expensive out here." "I want my son to be a doctor, then he can treat me for free." "My child should be an engineer or businessman, or whatever else that will fetch us enough money to keep us out of worries."

Paul asked a man, "So you work now so that later you could enjoy the fruits of your labor?"

"Makes sense, no? I will not be able to work when I am old. That is what my father did too. And his father. From ancient times. I am just upholding the tradition, no?"

"So you are OK to postpone the enjoyment of life?"

"Better postponed than never get, no?"

This man had a lot of faith in time tested norms. He had no need to try something else. In fact Paul's questions seemed to irritate him, as though answering would make him think, and he dreaded to think. Paul talked to his father. Was he enjoying life at last? No. His body ached. All he could do was read the newspaper and keep an eye on his grandchildren.

Satyen explained that most people work to keep the body-heart-mind engine running. And where was this engine taking them? Not many had the luxury to ask. Some who did, did not ask. Only a rare few did ask. And yet it was a question of paramount importance. People lived for the future and forgot about the present. They stressed out now so that later they could relax. They compressed themselves tight to decompress later. Not realizing that while they are compressing they are losing elasticity.

"OK, I am asking the question – where am I going?" said Paul.

"Good, very good," replied Satyen.

"What do you mean 'very good'? Give me the answer."

"Your destination? You know it best. And if you are still unsure, keep asking; you will get the answer. Of course you have to ask the right person."

"Come Satyen, why are you playing with words? I believe you are the right person. That is why I am asking you."

Satyen laughed, "I am not the right person at all. The right person is within you. We have many persons inside, so beware whom you question. They will all be eager to answer you. You will be misled if you heed them all. Find your inner being and listen to what it says."

Chapter Eight

Delight

Paul saw Hiren working away on a plot of land. He was planting saplings. Paul had never seen Hiren do a mundane task, so he asked, full of expectation, "Hiren, is there some mystery hidden here?"

"Of course! Inert soil, inorganic water and intangible sunlight create life. Have you seen a bigger mystery?"

"Hiren, I wanted some help. What am I supposed to do in life? I mean, what is the purpose of my life?"

Hiren looked up to read the degree of seriousness in Paul's question. He said, "Help me plant these."

When the two men were crouched head to head Hiren said, "Each of us has to ask that question to our innermost being. I cannot answer it for you."

"So it's not as simple as – go back to your country and run your company?"

"You are talking about your occupation. This is not an interesting question. But the one about your pre-occupation – now, that is the interesting one."

Paul brooded over it, "So will I get no guidance from you?"

"You are always getting it. From me, from Satyen, from everybody you meet, from the seasons, from the earth, from birds, from clouds, from everything that happens to you."

"Don't speak in riddles. What if I were a child asking. How would you answer? The question is: why do we live?"

"To have fun."

Paul almost dropped the tool, "Are you serious?" He suspected Hiren was teasing him.

Hiren answered, "Fun has an enormous range. At one end there are cheap thrills that last a short while and don't touch us very deep. Like eating food. Ingest, digest, excrete. Over. At the other end there is a delight that arises from within the being. People in such a state are always joyful, whether they get what they want or not. When the creator performed his miracle, his wand sent sparkles of delight all over his creation. There, you see it?"

Hiren pointed at the water gushing out of the jerry can. Paul saw the sparkles of light arching their way out of the spout and landing on the earth. Little golden droplets of heat trapped in the earth oozed out and evaporated. The green stems of the plants were translucent and he saw every cell in them reflecting back a luster. The fruits in the mango tree tickled by the caress of the breeze began to laugh. He looked at the boys in the street passing around a pebble, keeping it in the air by deft movements of the feet. Their faces were full of light and laughter. Their mothers sat nearby splitting big stones with hammers. They paused in their work to look at the children; and they smiled. The stray dogs weaved around their legs eager to be part of the game. The birds rose up from a tree all together. They had seen an eagle soar above. The eagle traced a large arc and pierced the clouds. It was a dance choreographed in detail. Every object he saw sank in his heart and caused ripples of laughter. Wave after wave of delight washed over him and surged out from his eyes as tears.

Hiren's voice floated in his ears, "Even in their despondency people don't forget to be happy. It is a primal instinct – to reach out for joy. This yearning is at the backdrop of even anxiety and pain. Even the simple life-forms such as flowers and trees exist for delight. The stone, the clod, the tools you use, they too have a sense in them. And this sense expresses delight. Everything that is created was conceived in delight, is sustained by delight, at the end returns to delight."

"Then why is there pain at all?"
"Because that too is a form of delight. The delight in experiencing the opposite of delight. The creator is a child playing with his toys. Some toys express love, some hatred, and he puts them together. He claps his hand when they collide. He claps his hand when they embrace. In victory he delights, in defeat he delights. He is bound by no action; he is free to take up any action. He is free to experience pain in delight and delight in pain. Seated in the heart of his creatures he experiences everything."

Every word Hiren spoke made sense within the fibers of Paul's being. The plant he had just tucked in the soil seemed to grow before his eyes. As it grew the leaves twisted around and offered themselves to the light. A bud took shape and it quivered in the air. Once, twice, thrice. Then there was a rupture in the skin and a pink petal emerged. And then another and another. Throwing the calyx backwards, the flower exposed itself to the light.
"Hiren!" cried out Paul, "Stop! I can't take it anymore. I am so full of delight I am going to burst."

They were walking on a desolate street, trees arching over their heads. Gradually the individual leaves started dancing to an insane rhythm. The trees became a green mass.

Paul asked, "If we are made of delight why don't we feel it all the time?"

"Because we forget. We who are children of immortality begin to believe ourselves to be mortal. We are circumscribed by our own limitations. Therefore say the wise, 'Remember, O soul, Remember!' If you remember to be happy can you also become free, because it means you are not being chased by your desires and jealousies and pride…"

"What of family and social duties? Do you get free from them too?"

Hiren laughed, "Freedom means non-attachment. You do everything you are bidden to do as long as you are bidden to do them. And who bids you to do? The divine. He knows what you need. If you need freedom from social bonds, he arranges it. If you need to serve society that too he arranges."

"Hiren, how did He arrange things for you? I am curious about your past. How did you come to the ashram? Will you tell me?"

Hiren laughed again. Paul signed, "I know, your external life is just a prop to help your soul's journey. My curiosity will remain unanswered."

"I will tell you. It is a story of little importance. Almost from the time I started to read, I pored over books.

Not the adventure stories other children read, but about the inner adventure. I did not play with them, but I practiced martial arts – the Indian style. I practiced meditation techniques. There was a man in town who guided me. I paid little attention to school and they rusticated me. Suited me well, as I could devote all my time to my practice. Did not suit my father. Toured quite a few schools and then father gave up. His rod did not rest though."

"Oh, so you have had your share of misery?"

"The body has had, no doubt. And hunger and cold and disease… Father was a regular man. Was thinking of his old age security plan. But fate solved it her own way. Died early of a sudden heart attack."

"Then the responsibility of your mother fell upon you?"

"Fate conspired again. When they were all shedding tears over father, I was calm. They thought I did not care for my father. I replied - all must die, and a death without suffering is a blessing. Mother was so distraught by her loss she called me a monster and threw me out of the house. See, I did not even have to struggle against family bonds. They set me free. I wandered around pilgrimage towns and people gave me alms. Had a few masters. Learnt new techniques. Had a few students. Never stopped long anywhere. When I reached here, I found I could concentrate on my work. Begging used to take up a lot of my time."

"Work? What is your work?" asked Paul breathless to hear the answer.

"Yoga, union with the Divine, perfection of the self...
There are many ways to say it, but in short, everything that
brings Delight. So you see, I live to have fun."

Chapter Nine

Flight

After a long hunt for Hiren Paul gave up. People had seen him walk towards the mango grove, but then his traces had vanished. Paul decided to use brute force. He screamed, "Hiren! Hiren!"

"Quiet, man! I almost lost my balance."

Paul heard Hiren's voice coming from somewhere close by, but the man was nowhere to be found. Then he looked up and saw Hiren seated on a stool he had balanced on the forking of a tree.

"What are you doing up there?"

"Practicing flying."

Paul wanted to say, "Funny", but he knew in Hiren's case it may be true.

"Are you doing a thought experiment?" he asked.

"No, it's a real experience."

"Can you prove it to me?"

"That depends on you. The perceiver needs the right tools of perception."

"Then nothing stops me from walking away thinking you are a fool on a stool."

"And why should I care about what you think of me?"

"Oh, come on, Hiren, give me some proof."

"Will describing what I see while I fly work?"

"Will work." Paul felt a thrill run through his limbs.

"Come on up here then. You will be able to see some of the things I will describe."

Chapter 9

Paul rested on a niche higher than Hiren and waited. Hiren sat in the lotus posture and closed his eyes. His chest heaved up and down in slow waves. The breaths became longer; the chest movements less pronounced. Then his body became immobile. Hiren started talking.

"I am rising above the branches and detaching myself from the tree. I skim the tree tops and feel the leaves tickle my chest and feet. Now I am above the row of tenements. A woman is hanging wet clothes in her balcony."

Paul could see the row of tenement homes, and yes, one of the balconies had a woman reaching up to the clothes line.

"I gain some elevation. I can see the ashram buildings and the paper mill. The river is coming up, rather brown and muddy. Must be because of the rain clouds above my head. What an inspiring sight - a flock of white herons against the grey sky."

Paul looked at the formation of white herons in the sky and wished he too could fly.

"I am carried up by a vortex. A hawk has caught the winds too. I fly towards the bird. Oh, but it is gone! It has swooped down to catch something in the grass. Now, what is this sound? I see – it is a kite. Someone is pulling it and the paper is making a rasping sound in the wind. I hope it does not tear. But maybe it is this way for kites all the time. From down there they look serene."

Paul spotted the red kite against the grey cloudy backdrop, floating gently across the sky.

"Why does that dog look up at me? Can he see me? Or does he simply sense something unusual? Now it is barking."

Paul strained his ears. Was that a distant barking he was hearing?

"A man standing nearby shouts at it. The dog is still barking. The man pretends to pick a stone and throws it at the dog. The dog cowers away. I have reached the river's edge. There is a boat on the river. Maybe I could fly to it."

The river shimmered far away tracing a silver line. Paul tried to spot the boat. He missed his binoculars. But what was the use? He believed everything Hiren said.

Hiren dismissed Paul's questions with one word, "Siddhi. This body is full of mysteries; not just mine; everybody's."
"Do you rise vertically?"
"Sometimes."
"Do you stretch out your hands like an airplane?"
"That should work too."
"Do you swim in the air?"
"In the beginning I used to do the breast stroke."
"Loosen up, Hiren, tell me more."
"Haven't you flown in your dreams?"
"Rarely. I wish I could do it on demand. Is it like that?"
"Somewhat, only much more concrete."

Chapter 9

"Let me tell you a story," said Hiren jumping off the tree. Paul landed beside him. "Once there was a hunter of birds. He caught peacocks for the feudal lord, parrots for trainers, bulbuls and mynas he sold as pets, and of course he caught the birds that were bought for their flesh. After some time people observed he had started behaving oddly. Instead of selling the birds he caught he used to pluck their feathers. Not all the feathers, just some. Then he would place the bird on various heights and observe their efforts at flight.

He had caught the ancient bug of flying. He did not tell anyone what he was experimenting. He was not the social type, so no-one asked. But his family suffered. He stopped bringing money home. Instead of catching birds he started caring for the injured ones who could not fly. One particular bird, a hawk, became quite attached to him. The two used to go out to the top of the hill. There he placed the bird on a slingshot and hurled it into the air. The poor thing uttered a wild cry and began to fall. It flapped its wings desperately and managed to stay in the air just long enough to dampen its fall. Then it flew back to the hunter and was launched again.

The village boys followed him and hid themselves behind rocks. They reported back his eccentricities. Then one day the bird flapped its wings as usual but instead of landing on the ground it started flying. It traced a large circle above the hunter's head. Man and bird were both immensely happy.

Flight

Every evening the hunter returned home and got a mouthful of his wife's abuses. But what can a man do when the heavens call him? He wanted to fly.

He too started off as a modern day scientist. He knew the exact number of feathers a bird required to fly. It depended on various factors, such as the species of bird, the amount of initial thrust, wind speed, air density, and so on.

The hunter had begun to spend his entire day at the riverside. He would observe the hawk skim over the water, wing tips touching the water's skin. The hunter's body did not move; he was frozen on spot. The boys were after him again, teasing him about his idleness, using the abuses they had learnt from his wife. But the hunter appeared to have become deaf towards them.

One day the boys thought they would play a prank. They crept behind him and pushed him over the bank. With a splash the man fell in, but strangely did absolutely nothing to save himself, not even thrashing his limbs about. Then the boys were dreadfully scared. Surely the man was alive, yet how is it that he would not save himself? And now he would surely drown. They ran back to the village and told the first person they met what had happened. One by one people started gathering at the riverside. Some people dived in but could not locate him. There was a slight current.

Then they saw a strange sight. The hawk was returning. It was flying at great speed. Somewhere upriver the bird plunged into the water. And it too disappeared without a struggle. Then men swam to the spot. At the bottom of the river they found man and bird – both were dead.

The story became a legend and was passed down the generations. Since nobody understood what had happened originally, subsequent generations believed it to be mere folklore."

Paul asked, "Let me guess. You believe it to be true because you *know* what had happened to the hunter."

"Yes, you are right."

"So, what had happened to the hunter?"

"Leave it. You will not believe it."

"I believe you flew today. Is that sufficient proof of my credulity?"

"Let's go to the riverbank."

Hiren and Paul sat on the river's edge and watched the breeze create gentle waves. Finally Hiren started speaking, "The hunter had found a way to identify his consciousness with the bird. He had studied flight, but his body was too heavy for flight. So he worked on transferring his consciousness into another's body. The hawk became his friend and started trusting him. When his consciousness penetrated into the body of the hawk, it allowed him. That is why he was not in his body seated by the riverbank that day. The body breathed mechanically, but it had no awareness. We call it a trance. This is another kind of out-of-body experience.

Then when his body was in danger, the consciousness felt a tug. I would hate to be in that poor man's place - flying back desperately to save his body. After all he could not live inside that bird forever, being human. When he sensed the body was dead, he had to unite himself with it, no matter what. That is why the bird chose to drown itself. This phenomenon of entering into another body is a power yogis develop. Somehow the hunter stumbled upon it. Who knows, maybe he was practicing yoga."

"Is that how you fly too?"
"No. Didn't you observe me speaking to you? So I was in control of my body. I used a different technique. I flew in my subtle body."
"I suppose it is weightless?"
"I cannot say, but it is lighter for sure. Have you heard of Milarepa, the Tibetan monk? Some people saw him flying in the sky. Of course these people may have had the vision of the subtle world. The gross world you apprehend with your senses is just one of the many worlds. Yoga opens up many new dimensions. It is an adventure for kingly spirits. More exciting than any exploration on the earth. More fulfilling than mental gymnastics. And gives you more exercise than martial arts. Yoga can make humans something more than what we currently understand as 'being human'."

Chapter Ten

Yoga

"One, two, three," counted a chorus of voices while Paul lay on his back in the sand pit. All he had to do was endure till ten. "Five, six, seven." Gopi, the heaviest member of the wrestling group, was sitting one him applying all his weight on Paul's shoulders. If the shoulders touched the ground Gopi would win the match. Paul concentrated on his shoulders and thought how nice it would be not to lose. Gopi was much heavier than him, but as they were of the same height Paul had to wrestle with him. The tournament was grueling, unlike the practice sessions. Ten minutes seemed like hours. Then Paul heard a voice addressing him, "Don't give up, there will be a challenge match if it is a draw."

This voice was encouraging him throughout the match. One advice it repeated several times, "Use the first lesson of yoga." Paul knew all the stunts involved in Indian wrestling and applied as many as he could, but the first lesson of yoga he had never been taught.

The voices rose to a crescendo, "Nine, ten!" Gopi relaxed his hold on Paul's shoulders and got up. It was a draw. Not many had the courage to fight Gopi, and hardly anyone drew against him. He grunted once, then grinning slapped Paul on the shoulder, "Well done! We meet again this afternoon."

Paul collapsed on the lawn and made no effort to watch the next pair. But when someone approached him and said, "Good show, Paul. Finally Gopi met a challenge." Paul sat up. This was the voice that was advising him. Paul drew him aside and thanked him for his much needed encouragements, "I heard your advice too. But it made no sense to me. I could not connect yoga and wrestling. Maybe I missed that lesson?"

Gautam looked at Paul surprised, "Really, you don't know what it means? But I have seen you with Hiren and Satyen so many times. Surely they have talked to you about yoga?"

"Yes, they did tell me what yoga is. I saw many fantastic things it can do, but I don't believe I learnt it in a methodical way."

"Come to think of it, Hiren and Satyen are not for novices. When we reach a peak and look up we see them standing far away on some high summit. Who knows how many lifetimes I will need to reach that far! You would have *experienced* what yoga can do, but you would not *know* how to get there. Is that somewhat right?"

"You are absolutely right."

Gautam and Paul walked around the garden while the other pairs engaged in their ten minute wrestling matches. Gautam said, "The first lesson you learn when you start the journey of the discovery of the Self is that there are many paths to get there. You choose the path that comes easiest to you. In other words you use your God given gifts. As I see it in wrestling your gift is swiftness.

Gopi's is his weight. If you are fast you can tip his balance and then get out of the way. Let gravity do the rest. He will fall and then again using your swiftness you must pin his shoulders to the ground before he can react. Once he gets back his balance even if you sit on him he can easily shrug you off."

Gautam made Paul practice his moves until he was so swift the eye could hardly follow him. Then Paul was back in the sandpit picking up a bit of sand and bowing to it. Gopi slapped his copious thighs to intimidate his opponent. Usually in the first few seconds the two combatants face each other and move in a circle waiting to lunge in. But this time Gopi had not even finished slapping his thighs when both his legs were pulled forward. He landed on his back with a mighty thud. Immediately Paul's palms were pinning his shoulders down. A split second later Gopi turned over on his stomach. Paul tried to roll him over but it was impossible. He jumped out of Gopi's way and waited. Gopi got up and looked at Paul, slightly less confident now. The onlookers were clapping.

The two circled each other, their faces thrust forward. Gopi was breathing hard; the fall did not do him any good. Paul kept telling himself, "You are fast, remember. You can do it only if you act suddenly." And so he did. Gopi was surprised a second time. Paul fell to the ground and wedged his legs between Gopi's massive legs. One twist and he executed the scissors stunt. Gopi lost his balance and crashed to the ground on his side. Paul rolled him over and this time managed to pin his shoulders to the ground. Gopi's fall had left him disoriented for just that long. The bell rang and Paul jumped to his feet. He had won!

"Gautam, you are a savior!" cried Paul.
"No, you are a good learner. Congratulations!"
"I can't wait to learn some more. What is the second lesson? I am so excited. You know, I must confess, before I came here I had a completely different idea of progress. It meant making more money, attracting more friends, throwing bigger parties, having more cars. But now I realize it has nothing to do with the outer circumstances. And everything to do with what we truly are."

"You already know the next steps then. They can be answered by asking three questions. Do you really want a better life? If the answer is yes you are already aspiring. How do I get there? By rejecting all the lower movements. And whom do I ask for help? Not your ego, but some higher power. You develop faith. You surrender to it.

Aspiration, rejection, surrender. You aspire for a better life. You reject whatever stands in your way. You surrender to the higher power to guide you. Now you can ask me, 'what do these words really mean in terms of practice?' And here I will remind you of the first lesson. Use your inherent strength. Swiftness was your physical strength. Similarly you have a strength you can use to practice yoga."

"What do you see as my strength?"

"Well, that is hard for me to tell. But I can tell you what my strength is, as an example. My path is the path of knowledge. I am a mental person. When I meditate I work on my mind. To aspire I need to read wisdom texts. While I read I can feel myself yearning to become more spiritual. I seek to be transformed and I pray to the higher power to help me. That is the surrender. As for rejection when I am reading I am not thinking negative thoughts. The knowledge I am gathering helps me understand myself better. I can then reject what is not noble. So you see how the three tie in my practice of yoga?

But the path of knowledge is just one of the paths. There are people who use work as the main method of yoga. They offer their work to the divine…"

"And not worry about the results," Paul continued Gautam's thought.

"Yes, that is right. And then there is the path of emotions. People who have a strong heart center use the path of devotion. They trust the divine, their friend and lover, to do whatever is best for them. There are other paths too. Each stresses on some aspect of our nature. As novices we choose the path that suits us best. Eventually we must do them all."

"Were you sure of your path from the beginning or did you try a few and then pick this one?"

"In my case I was sure of my path. Of course I am practicing the path of works too. I teach science at the school in town. I had always been a good student and I loved physics and math in school. I worshipped science. I thought spirituality was humbug. I used to challenge the elderly and ask them to prove to me why they thought God existed, why they said He helped them, and so on. Later I realized there can be no dispute between science and spirituality."

"Really? How is that?"

"They play by different rules. Science asserts a truth should be testable. But that begs a question. What instruments are you using to test? If you have coarse instruments obviously you cannot measure the subtle. Science does not yet have adequate instruments to measure truth. Secondly science speaks in terms of quantities. But spirituality talks in terms of infinities. Do you see the disconnect?

Science is like a child who has just learnt 'two plus two'. Obviously it will not understand the language of calculus. It needs to grow up. The rational mind is a trouble-maker compared to the higher mind. Of course we cannot get rid of it unless we have that better mind at our command. But it is good to know that it is a clerk. It should not be treated as a master. If you can silence it you start *knowing* things, *hearing* things, *seeing* things. That is what I have been told. I am not there yet. In fact by one definition yoga is the cessation of mental activities.

Spirituality is a superset, science the subset. The superset can understand the subset. Not the other way around. The dispute arises when the subset thinks it is the biggest set. A little humility is all it takes."

"If you will allow me to remark, from your story is sounds like that humility was lacking to start with."

"Of course you can make that remark. And you are right. I was one arrogant fool who was put in his place one fine day. I will tell you how it happened. It helps to know other people's mistakes - saves us the trouble of repeating them.

I was in my final year at school, just before going to college. We had a project to make something out of scrap metal. We could take the entire year to do it and at the end we would be judged and given out prizes. I made a battleship. It had a runway for fighter jets, some fighter jets, a row of mounted guns, several decks at different levels, cannons... It was full of details. I used to go to the junk yard where they dump electronics and cars and pick up little pieces of scrap.

At the end of the school year we sat before a stage where our artworks were placed covered by paper hoods. All the students were present and our parents too. One by one they uncovered the artworks and people cheered the artist. Then the three remained that would win prizes. Mine was there and I could hardly sit still. The third prize was given and mine was still there on the stage. Then they uncovered the second prize. And it wasn't mine. But as I looked at it something started happening inside me.

She had made a Buddha. The curls of his hair were soda bottle caps hammered into domes. His robe was silver. She had pasted tin foil on it, taken from cigarette packets. His body was copper made of electrical wires hammered flat and held together by some more copper wire. The statue was so beautiful everyone praised it. And I thought to myself, "Look at what I have done with my skill. I have made an object of destruction. For one year while this girl was filling her mind with the thoughts of a saint, I was cramming it with war."

They had uncovered my ship and were calling out my name. Everybody was clapping. I marched up to the stage, lifted my ship above my head and dropped it on the floor. It fell with a terrible crash and lay in a broken heap. Bits and pieces of metal rolled away. Some gasped and then there was complete silence. I held my prize, a cup, and called the girl who had made the Buddha. She was standing on the stage along with my other classmates. I gave her my cup. She was confused, looked at the judges. Then she accepted it and wanted to give her prize to me. But I walked out of the room. Ever since I have been a different person."

Chapter Eleven

Tiger

A page from Paul's diary:

Hiren had the goat slung over his shoulders and I was carrying a wooden plank and some rope. It was morning but the forest was dark and sinister. Monkeys swung from branches and they did not like us trespassing. I was ready to give in if Hiren would suggest turning back. But he kept marching ahead crunching the dry leaves under his feet. I think the goat fell asleep on his shoulders. Suddenly we were startled by a flood of light. We had reached a clearing where a few trees had fallen, struck by lightning.

Hiren tied the goat to one of the charred stumps and looked for a tree. We climbed and placed my plank between two branches. I sat down and for further precaution tied myself to the branch with the rope. Hiren leapt down and waited beside the goat and I waited in my watch tower. Mosquitoes flew around but all I could do was squeeze them with my fingers. No human sound should be heard in the forest, I was told.

After an hour or so I heard a distant crunching of leaves. It came closer and I knew it was from a heavy beast. I hoped it would be a tiger. Hiren had risen silently and was waiting in front of the goat facing the crunching sound. The goat started bleating; at first in uncertain bursts, then in a steady terrified cry. The footfall approached rapidly and in a split second a creature emerged into the clearing under me. It was a tiger, muscles rippling, stripes of gold and black glistening, a sight that almost made me scream in awe and fright.

For a moment it looked up at Hiren; then it spotted the goat. It made for the goat ignoring the man. Then it was as amazed as myself, seeing the man rush towards it fearlessly. Hiren dug his hands under the creature's belly and turned it on its back with a swift movement. The tiger sprang up and leaped into the air uttering a chilling roar. I hid my face in my hands gasping for breath. But just for a fraction of a second. Then through my fingers what I saw made me sick of terror. If my tongue had not stuck to my palate I would have screamed.

Hiren stamped on the ground hard and launched himself into the air to meet the tiger head on. Or so I thought. But Hiren and the tiger crossed each other without contact. As soon as they landed they both turned around and were facing each other. The tiger charged forward. Hiren planted his hands on its shoulders and arrested its motion. The tiger roared in fury, so close to Hiren's ear I thought he would collapse with the impact of the sound. But no, he responded with a loud "Hum!" and pushed the tiger away.

The incredulous beast charged again and this time aimed at planting its teeth into Hiren's head. But Hiren moved so fast it did not know what hit it on the side. The tiger travelled through the air and landed on the ground with a loud thud. This time is scrambled up and made for the goat. But it could not move forward. Hiren's foot was on its tail. It simply did not make sense that a mere human could restrain such a big tiger.

The tiger struggled to get away. Then it whirled around, mouth wide open, ready to clamp its jaws on its tormentor. But Hiren ran around holding the tail in his hand. The two went around in circles so fast my head was spinning. I was afraid any moment Hiren would lose the race and then it would be all over. I wished he had brought at least his stick. As for me I wanted to get an axe, but he forbade me.

But of the two the tiger was tiring faster. It was now tottering, its head in a muddle. Hiren had left the tail and watched it take a few unsteady steps. Then he knelt down and placing his hands under the belly, he lifted the tiger. Clean and jerk. Right above his head. I thought I was going to faint. From my position all I could see was the tiger stretched out helplessly. Before it could react Hiren had thrown it against a tree. The tree shook and many leaves fell to the ground. Had it been my tree I would have been on the ground for sure.

The tiger was hurt, but not dispirited. It uttered a humiliated cry and ran for Hiren. Again Hiren was under it. He did it so fast I could not even follow his movement. A second time the tiger was hurled. Then a third. Each time the tiger seemed weakened by the blow. But it returned, incredulous of the defeat.

Finally the tiger gave up. I heard it run away. The crunching sound became faint and all was quiet again. I exhaled and leaned against the branch. Hiren climbed up beside me with the goat. He cautioned me to keep still. The goat had shivered so much in fright it was sweating. All it could do was lay its head on the plank and pass out. We waited for another hour. Then we returned to the village.

My head was bursting with questions, but Hiren walked ahead with the goat on his shoulders and would not let me catch up. He seemed to enjoy my pain. Finally I ran for him and caught up. As I had suspected, he was smiling. He wasn't even scratched. That is how skillfully he had maneuvered the tiger with its inch-long lethal claws. Not to mention the terrifying roar and that open mouth full of fangs. I didn't even know how to formulate my questions.

I asked, "So how did you do it?"
"I was wrestling with Gopi the other day. And since I could lift him above my head I wanted to try something heavier."
"Alright, then why didn't you lift the water buffalo we see grazing by the pool? That fellow is heavy."
"But that fellow is docile. He is hardly a challenge."
"Why a tiger, of all creatures! The temple has an elephant if you wanted a good challenge. Try lifting that fellow."
"I would not hurt a tame creature. I wanted some wild thing. Did you see the tiger's courage? Unmatched in the animal kingdom. I have to concentrate hard to fill my body with that sort of strength. If I am doing it, why not go to the extreme?"

"If I get nightmares tonight, just you watch. I will not let you sleep either. But how is it that the tiger could not push you back after it applied all its body weight against you? Did you also become that heavy?"

"I was strong enough to counter its weight. This isn't muscular strength. It is another kind of strength. Your rational mind will not be able to understand, but your senses have not lied. This is possible. Our legends are full of such stories. Yours too. Hercules performs similar feats. The body has so many hidden powers. There is so much more we can do if only we allow it. It's the rational mind that is the biggest hurdle. It doubts, disbelieves, discourages. Quieten it and let the higher powers come into play. They will lead you on to such discoveries you will wonder how you had lived so far without them. You will again wake up with wonder in your eyes as you did when you were a child."

Chapter Twelve

Shield

Paul woke up feeling uncomfortably hot. The mattress was wet with his sweat. He curled up on the floor heavy with sleep. But he could get no sleep. Soon he found out why. With his ear on the floor he could hear sounds coming from the room below. What was under his room? He suddenly woke up alert. It was the room with the gods and goddesses. What could be happening there at this hour? He looked at his watch, it was around midnight.

He walked down the stairs hesitantly. He did not want to meet any fantastic being alone at night. But he was curious too. It was a pitch dark night with no moon in sight. The meditation hall's windows were shut as usual. Paul crept close to the shutter and placed his ear against it. Sure enough there was something happening inside the room. The shutters vibrated. He poked a trembling finger and made a chink in the shutter. All he could see was a lamp dancing about madly. He was about to utter a terrified cry when he checked himself. He had seen something else in the dark. A man was holding that lamp and dancing with it. The man faced the gods and goddesses. His steps were nimble, his body agile. Paul could have easily guessed who it was, but at that very moment the man turned around in his dance and Paul saw Hiren's face.

In his left hand he held an earthen pot, just big enough to fit his palm. His right wrist made wiggly gestures that gave the lamp a wave-like trajectory. He was muttering something. Paul felt ashamed to steal up on someone's private ritual, but the dance was so magnificent he was transfixed. Leaping up Hiren landed doe-like on the balls of his feet. Then arching his back he whirled the pot around his head.

Paul watched him unblinking for a while. Then he crept upstairs and wrote in his diary what he had just witnessed. The page was full of exclamation marks. He had seen a ritual worship before but it was plain compared to this dance. This was Shiva's tandava.

He thought he had slept just a wink when someone knocked on his door. It was Hiren. Paul was about to say how impressed he was last night when he checked himself. Hiren should not know he was eavesdropping. Hiren said, "Come, today's sunrise is special. I want to show you something."

They walked to the terrace and Hiren instructed Paul to look at the rising sun without blinking. Hiren held his temples from the back and pressed on them. "Do you see any colors?" asked Hiren. "No," replied Paul. After some time again Hiren asked the same question. The sun was rising over the horizon and it wasn't a cloudy day that made the sky a spectacle worth watching. Paul could not see anything special. After a few trials Hiren said, "You are not too open for an experience now. We'll try some other time. Go to sleep."
Paul returned to his room and immediately fell into a deep sleep.

After lunch Satyen asked Paul what he was planning to do that evening. "Nothing special."

"You could come to the tribunal. You will probably not understand anything, but you will get an idea of what *else* we do here in the ashram."

"What tribunal?"

"Hiren's."

"What's happening? Listen, maybe tribunal means something else here."

"No, it means the same thing."

All the brothers of the ashram were seated in the meditation hall. Hiren entered and seeing Paul asked him what he was doing there. His tone was friendly. Satyen answered saying *he* had invited Paul for the tribunal. Hiren kept quiet. Some younger brothers fidgeted. Nobody spoke. Everybody waited for someone else to begin speaking. Tribunals were not common Paul guessed. And Hiren was their instructor in so many ways.

Satyen finally broke the silence. He explained that some brothers felt he was not focusing on the goals of the ashram. He was spending too much time on developing his powers. Hiren defended his motives of experimenting with yogic powers. A brother said, "Some people also suspect you are starting your own teaching program here. A student learns at his own pace; he is not to be pushed or gifted an experience."

Paul felt sick. Was *he* the reason why Hiren was on trial? Then someone brought up Nisha. Was he just helping her or was there more to it? Hiren lost his calm for a minute, "A woman is always suspect irrespective of the nature of interaction! Nisha needs direction in life. If she finds my advice helpful, should I be blamed for it?"

"How is it that she comes to you alone?"

"Maybe you should ask *her* why she does not consult with anyone else."

Satyen wanted Hiren to elaborate on the nature of his help. Hiren said there was nothing to elaborate. To which Satyen said if he was so sure of his right conduct why did he wear the kavach? Some of the brothers were visibly startled when they heard the word. Hiren did not deny it, which meant he was wearing the kavach. Satyen and Hiren went on about the kavach and Paul wished he could interrupt someone and ask what it meant.

Hiren asked, "My kavach would not affect you if you did not want to read my mind. And if you had anyway planned to read my mind why did you set up a tribunal?"

Satyen replied, "I am not the only one here who wants to talk to you about where you are headed. Besides I am not trying to probe into your mind. I trust what you say. This is not a trial in a courtroom; it is a friendly discussion. So there is no need to speak guardedly. We are a family of aspirants and it is best to be candid about everything. That you felt a kavach was necessary makes me rather sad. Better we meet some other time when you can trust us." Another date was fixed.

Satyen said he needed fresh air and pulled Paul away with him.

"What is a kavach?" asked Paul as soon as he could.

"A shield. Hiren has created a shield around himself and I could not read him - mind, heart, anything."

"Why did you try? He is right to feel hurt."

"I don't try. These are faculties I have. Think of the blind; how they have extended the sense of touch to read braille. Similarly mental faculties can be extended in various ways. But what I saw today was this opaque cocoon within which he was seated. Frankly this very action of his makes me suspicious."

"Do you think he has something with Nisha?"

"Not me. But some of the junior brothers have been wondering. They think he gets more privileges. I am not blaming them. It is not easy to conquer the Darwinian instinct. But listen, you are often with Hiren. Did you notice anything odd about him lately?"

"Odd? Let me think. Actually, yes, this very morning. He woke me up early this morning, said it was a special sunrise and took me to the terrace. I was supposed to see some colors when the sun rose. He pressed my temples but ..."

Satyen stopped him abruptly, "He pressed your temples?"

"Yes, why? Does that mean something to you?"

"What do you remember before that? Were you with him yesterday?"

Paul shrugged, he could not remember. Satyen said, "Let me tell you what happened. He erased your memory. Some part of your memory. Something he wanted me not to read. He knows I can read your mind."

"So you can? Thank you for allowing me my privacy."

"Don't worry, I don't read your mind. But if I wanted I could. This is serious. I wish I knew what he erased. The sunrise was just an alibi."

Suddenly Paul thought of something. "If there was anything unusual I may have written it down in my diary. Maybe it is there."

The two returned to the ashram. And sure enough something had been written down. Paul read his own diary as though it was someone else's experience. He searched his memory, but the magnificent dance of Hiren's was nowhere to be found.

Paul frowned, "I wonder how he knew I was there. Oh, never mind the question."

Satyen was nodding his head wisely.

"What is it?" asked Paul.

"As I had suspected, he made himself a kavach of Goddess Kali."

"How do you know?"

"That pot is the symbol of the Goddess. It represents the womb, the receptacle that holds the divine seed. And midnight is Kali's hour."

"Did I just put Hiren in trouble?"

"He has cornered himself. Wearing such a powerful kavach against us wasn't wise. These powers have a life of their own."

"But surely Hiren is capable of controlling it?" asked Paul, worried.

"I hope so," replied Satyen, but his tone was unsettling.

Chapter Thirteen

Shadows

It was impossible that Hiren was undergoing a trial, Paul thought to himself. A person who could reveal a great truth by simply uttering a few words was master of himself. And what a powerful energy he had! Paul could not, would not, allow Hiren to be insulted. There must have been some misunderstanding. Maybe Satyen did not know Hiren's work.

Paul found Satyen alone the next morning and cornered him. He was almost aggressive, "Hiren gave me the answer. The purpose of the creation is Delight. And Hiren *is* delight. He could not have gone wrong. His work is to spread delight and I have seen him do it to me."

Satyen's response was a chuckle, "He has power to spread whatever he likes. For example confusion - if that was what he wanted you to experience. He chose delight for you."

"But Satyen, this is exactly what I am saying too. He will not choose the wrong thing."

"Power has a life of its own. He can fight wild beasts, he can fly, he can see the future, plant thoughts in people's minds, direct their actions. But what does he do with all that power? Performs miracles! Like a rich man getting richer, he multiplies his powers. The body, heart and mind are instruments – like a car. The soul is the master. It owns the car; it is not the car. You can have a sophisticated car or a simple one, but the point is to get from one place to another. If you lose focus of your destination, you can get lost in a scenic route."

Paul held his peace. Satyen's tongue had loosened and now was not the time to interrupt.

"He is concentrating too much on perfecting his instruments; going an extra mile even. That is all very good if these are peripheral activities. The main purpose of being an instrument of the divine gets lost if one is too eager to accomplish one's own goals." Satyen paused, "I suppose I did not tell you that our purpose is to be available for the Divine?"

Paul shook his head, "No, but new ideas do not surprise me anymore."

"Good, then I can try to explain. There is a Will of the Divine out there for us. And we have our desires out here. His Will and our desires may not be aligned. The Will knows what is best for us. It has a clear vision of our spiritual journey. Our desires draw us away from that path. When we can eliminate our desires then there is a chance we can follow the Will.

Consider this example: you have to cross a mountain pass. There is a tightrope connecting the two peaks. Your coach is giving you instructions. But if you are deaf or blind or lame even if you are willing you cannot walk on the tightrope. So you have to develop your instruments - ears, eyes, limbs - to become fit for the task."

"But here can I ask, why do I have to cross the mountain pass?"

"Because your coach wants you to. He wants you to climb new peaks. That is what progress is all about. Discovering new heights. If he was your parent he would fear for you and not let you attempt the dangerous journey. As you grow you will know his intentions. But in elementary school your mind is not ready to grasp it."

"And Hiren's mind?"

"Is too ready, so ready he has outsmarted the Will and missed the mark. All I am trying to convey to him is this: a person of his ability should not waste time being a magician. He is a yogi. You know, Hiren means 'diamond'. At some point he must realize he is a diamond, not a magnet.

Positive qualities too can have a shadow of their own. Take love - human love. Starts off pure; then brings its shadow of attachment, shortly followed by jealousy, possessiveness, betrayal, suffering, hatred. A mother who cares too much could stunt her child's growth. She could as well break his leg to be sure he will never climb a tree. Take the ideals of activists, philanthropic doctors, or peace workers. A small voice asks them – what is there for *me* in it? And the shadow enlarges itself and one day looms larger than the ideal. Look at statecraft – communism came with its shadow of dictatorship, capitalism has its shadow of selfishness, democracy has the cheapest ideas voted in.

Power has its shadow too. A powerful person wants control. Hiren loves to show miracles to people. It may have taken you a whole lifetime to see Delight as the bedrock of creation. But he gifted you that vision in one afternoon. Did you deserve that knowledge? Will you value it now that it came to you so easily? You have missed the thrill of the journey, the joy of working out a complex problem by yourself. It isn't enough to have reached. There are nuggets on the way you have missed picking."

Paul kept quiet. He was thinking of his father's good intentions that brought him to India. Did it perhaps hide a shadow too? He asked, "How do I catch a shadow in a good intention?"

"You can take a photograph of it every day and inspect it closely." Satyen spoke in riddles, but this one was a little too much for Paul. A concrete example would help. He said, "I was thinking of my father's good intention of sending me here."

Satyen explained, "Say you are building a pier. How far should you extend it into the sea? You need to know the number of freights coming in, their size, the shallowness of the water, etc. And how can you know these if you do not stand way above and take a picture of the coastline?"

"I see, and I need to do it every day to get a good idea of the traffic over time."

"Inspect the image and you may find shadows where none should exist. Work on them. Some people keep a journal of their inner progress to achieve this. Like the diary you are writing. It helps to have a big picture. You need to step back from the individual events to see the trajectory your life is taking. There is a witness self within you that is sleeping. You can awaken it and use its vision to re-adjust the course of your life. It is not easy to observe oneself. Observe your thoughts, your intentions, your prejudices, your habits, your speech, your movements, your everything. You will then know it wasn't your father who sent you here. It was the guiding light that is watching over you; watching over all of us. The Divine Will. The best we can do is to be available; to be fit instruments of this Will."

Chapter Fourteen

Tribunal

A page from Paul's Diary:

I did not go to the second tribunal. Come to think of it, why did Satyen call me in the first place? I don't want to humiliate Hiren. He is one of my closest friends. No, more than a friend. He is my hero, my guide. I admire him, I adulate him. Is that why Satyen called me? So that *he* could replace Hiren in my esteem? No! What am I thinking? Satyen is above such sentiments. And who am I in the big picture?

They accused Hiren of not performing his duties because he had become too involved with magic. These powers are called siddhis. These are not supposed to be goals but just gifts on the way. As one works on self-perfection one is blessed with these gifts, such as inner hearing, seeing visions, having access to greater knowledge, and so on. Each one of us can get these.

Example: if you learn to swim you can cross a river. Will you call it a special power? Not anymore, because hundreds of people can do it. But what of the first man who did it? His kinsmen perhaps thought he would drown. But lo and behold, he floated on the surface and reached the other shore. They fell upon their knees and bowed low to him. He was crowned king in some civilizations, burnt at the stake in some others. But everybody acknowledged he had a power they did not possess. Maybe in some future date the powers of inner audition and mind reading would be commonplace.

Anyway let me not digress. Someday I wish to use this diary as notes for my inner pilgrimage. That is, when Satyen will not be there to guide me. Already Hiren is leaving. Yes, he is, I asked as many brothers as I could meet and they all said so. I don't know how it will be here without Hiren. So many days I have woken up wondering if Hiren would show me something new. Some technology that shames our hand-held devices and our universal connectivity. At best we are connected to people - loosely with those who don't speak our language, better with others. But here they can say when a fruit needs to be plucked because the fruit tells them so. The snakes that are poisonous become docile when they stray into the ashram. Untrained dogs follow orders. Birds lose their free will.

Again I digress. I did not go to the tribunal because the concepts discussed were way above my head. A man's integrity is being questioned. Integrity measured with a yardstick I cannot even begin to comprehend. Satyen told me what transpired. Hiren came in without the protection, the kavach. They scanned him using their X-Ray vision, MRI of the consciousness, things our technology has no clue of. They found a scarf around his neck, the kind women in India wear. I suspected it was Nisha's. Satyen laughed at me. He said it was not a real scarf. It was created by human emotions, in the aura."
"Surely Hiren knew about it?" I asked.

Satyen replied, "Hasn't it happened to you that sometimes you forget what you are wearing? We don't turn our eyes on ourselves often."

Hiren was cross questioned and he said he would be perfectly happy not to see Nisha again. His only regret was that the work he was doing with her would remain incomplete. She had a hurdle to cross, and someone else would have the pleasure of seeing her across it. Or maybe she would not cross it in this lifetime.

The congregation remained mostly silent. Their answers were in gestures such as hanging their heads or shaking them in agreement or disagreement. At the end Hiren said he needed to step back to look at himself, since he wasn't seeing what was apparent to the others. He admitted that perhaps he was heading the wrong way. Perhaps he was working too hard to gain powers. He had begun to think he mattered to Nisha. He was measuring his efforts in terms of results.

Now this beats me. How can you not have an eye on the results? You help this woman who needs your help, but you do it without regard to the outcome. If she learns something, good for her; if she does not, too bad. But you remain indifferent to it. Then how can you be interested to help her? Satyen corrected me when I asked him these questions. "You are not indifferent, but delighted. Both ways. Your delight is in trying. The results are not in your hands. A million things happen which are external to you. Even after you do your best you may not succeed because the universe or God or the Beneficence that cares for people has chosen otherwise. Or maybe failure is the best reward for you as it will teach you a lesson. What is helpful is to be prepared, rather than win once and learn nothing. Of course it is not necessary that you learn nothing when you win, but the winning or losing are aftereffects, not the real aim."

One thing I have come to accept. The results are not in our hands. Call it chance, freak accident, others meddling, or Divine Grace, but one has little control over the course of events. Big events. Not small ones such as will I get lunch today or will I return to the US. Big ones such as will my love for a person remain till the end? Will I keep striving for a better inner life?

Hiren chose his own punishment. It is not easy to live in this world without a shelter. This organization took care of his material needs. He could concentrate on his inner journey. And now he will be on his own, thinking about his next meal, wondering where he would rest. Will he get time to work on the real work? Will he be pushed to give up? Satyen told me if he got lucky he would find another ashram. In the old days he could find patronage from the neighboring king. But these days people don't see value in supporting hermits. Those whose outputs are intangible are hunted out of existence. If a family chooses to give him shelter, Hiren's presence can protect them, whether they know it or not - from calamities, bad will from others, even the hand of fate. Such is the greatness of

Hiren's consciousness. But he is greater still. He will not advertise himself.

Then why let him go? Satyen's lame excuse was, "He chose it himself. We spoke not a word. The tribunal is a process of self-searching. He uncovered his own self and shone his own light on it. It was a most successful tribunal. I would be happy if he chose to stay. Now that he is made aware he could begin concentrating on the real work. Even if he going he knows he can always return."

Here I was just beginning to learn about inner technology when I hear the lab has no funding for it. But wait a minute, Satyen, I think Hiren will find another lab. *I* will fund him. I will take him to America. He will never need to worry about material needs. And nobody will cross examine him.

Chapter Fifteen

Betrayal

Paul did not want to disturb Hiren yet. So he thought of doing the next important thing – give Nisha the bad news. He started hiking towards the forest. Half way through he met the lady herself. She was red in the face as she came hurriedly down the slope. "Paul," she paused to regain her breath, "Is it true?"

"I am afraid so."

"Is it too late?"

She broke into a run and Paul jogged along to keep up, "Listen, I don't think it's a good idea to disturb him now."

Nisha stopped briefly, "Disturb?" then she picked up speed again, "What an idea! Why should Hiren feel disturbed with me?"

Paul did not know how he could break the second piece of bad news to her. That she had a role to play in his exile - self-imposed, but exile nonetheless.

All he could do was sympathize, "I suppose you want to say goodbye."

Nisha's voice sounded like the stab of a knife, "That I will never say. In fact I am glad he is getting free of this place."

"You surprise me, isn't it a safe haven for a yogi?"

She scowled and hurried on.

"You don't like the ashram, I presume."

"That artificial habitat? No, I don't. And now I am glad Hiren can live in a more natural place. In fact I have an idea for him. That is why I want to talk to him."

"Well, it turns out that is exactly what I was thinking of doing. Take him to America with me and provide for everything he could need, materially speaking. I will set up classrooms where he can conduct spiritual classes and build a gym for him to teach martial arts. He will be a great counselor - I mean a spiritual coach."

She scoffed at him, "Make him wear a large orange turban and send him on lecture tours? And who would respect his teachings there? They would be scared of his kind of yoga. He does not teach contortions."

They were both sprinting now, competitors in a new challenge. Paul brought out his words panting, "You will be surprised how well he will be accepted. He can become a guru, like Yogananda or Vivekananda. Watch and see. I will launch him."

"While you are at it, make posters of the miracle-mongering guru, advertise on TV, roll the marketing machinery and flatten him out."

"Let's hear *your* brilliant idea for him."

"Brilliant or not, you cannot take him away. How would I live without him? I mean, I would not know how to function. He was my guide and still is."

"There are others who can guide you."

"No," she screamed, "It is and will have to be him."

Suddenly Paul realized either he was talking to one who had lost her mind or one who was in love. Maybe the two states were the same. He whistled softly and thought, so it was love after all. The scarf Satyen saw strung around Hiren was Nisha's love for him. Hiren did not see it, so he must have been ignorant of it. Maybe he was being punished for another's crime. And to be fair, it wasn't a crime. She wasn't a nun, why should she restrain her love? Surely she sees Hiren's release as a blessing. Paul needed to act fast. Hiren was misjudged. Maybe he could still remain in the ashram.

The two had reached the ashram and they made for Hiren's room.

Nisha knocked on the door, "It's me! Are you in?"

When they got no response they pushed on the door. It was locked from inside. Nisha ran to the window and peeped in. Suddenly she was hysterical. She hit her head against the window bars. She wailed and tears poured down her cheeks. Paul ran to her and looked in. "Oh my God!" he whispered and ran back to the door. He tried to force it open by applying his weight against it. Nisha cried out, "All is lost, I am finished."

Within seconds others came running to the spot and asked them the reason for the commotion. Paul gave orders, "Do you have screw drivers? We need to get the hinges out. Someone go to the toolshed."

Satyen arrived and asked Paul what was happening.

Dragging Satyen to the window Paul said, "Look at what you have all done to him." They saw Hiren's body seated on the bed slumped against the wall. His head was bent forward. He was unnaturally still.

Satyen lifted his hands and said one word to the crowd, "Shhh!" The brothers withdrew quietly. Satyen looked at Nisha, "If you want to cry so loudly at least step away from Hiren's hearing range."

"Are you crazy?" asked Paul, "Or simply heartless? Come on Satyen, do something before it is too late."

Satyen was firm, "You two are the crazy ones. Don't you know Hiren travels in his subtle body? Luckily your commotion has not jerked him back."

Paul was still agitated, "He sits on top of a tree when he does these exercises."

"Not in the evening. Too many mosquitos."

"Are you sure? How can you be so sure? He has suffered a shock - the tribunal, the verdict of exile."

"How little you know of Hiren. Even you, Nisha. I thought you would be wiser and not make a spectacle of your loss. You think Hiren is so bankrupt that he will give up his life for something so trivial? Paul, go to help in the kitchen. Nisha, go back to your hotel. It is getting dark, we will have dinner now."

Nisha's voice trembled as she spoke, "You can all go but I will stay right here till Hiren returns...to his normal state."

Paul followed Satyen, "Satyen, I must talk to you. It wasn't Hiren's fault. She loves him. She wants to take him with her. She sees this as an opportunity to strike. Hiren should stay here. He belongs here, the townsfolk need him."

"You mean, you don't want to collect your pot of gold?"

Paul wished he knew how to hide his thoughts. He shrugged, "Alright, I am keeping my hands off him. But if he does choose to leave, I don't see any harm in making my offer. Let him decide. It's not for money, you *know* that."

From the window of the dining hall they could see Nisha seated on the doorstep. "Poor girl, she must be hungry," thought Paul. Just then Hiren's door opened and Paul almost choked on his food. Hiren walked out. Nisha leaped to one side. They were talking. Then Nisha made a sudden move and clutched Hiren's feet with her hands. Paul looked around and saw several bothers had gathered at the window. Hiren and Nisha remained in that position for some time. They were conversing, or rather, negotiating. Paul looked at Satyen, who was eating nonplussed.

The brothers settled down as they saw Hiren walking towards the dining hall. Nisha sat on the doorstep her head between her knees, shaking and sobbing. She was still there as the evening prayers began. Inside the meditation hall Paul looked around for Hiren. He wasn't there. "Poor fellow, made his flight," he thought and sat down.

Someone strode in breathing so hard the meditators were hurried out of their calm. It was Nisha. She seized the yak tail whisk and set it on fire. Then whirling it above her head she spat on the floor, "You frauds, you think you control people's lives? You make them dance as though they were your puppets?" She beat her chest, "Today this puppet has torn her strings. Come get me before I spit on your hermitage." The brothers got up and stood staring at her. Bits of the burnt whisk flying in the air landed all around. When the whisk was just a stump she tossed it on the floor and made for the frankincense holder. Opening the lid she ran around sprinkling the scented ashes on the floor. The floor was a mess.

She jumped on the podium and seized the idols of Radha and Krishna, "You are scared of love but worship these two? Why? Poor fools! Let me rid you of this hypocrisy." She tore the clothes off the two idols and waved them in front of the audience. "See, how naked they can be. And oh, I see they have no genitals, no breasts. Theirs is a sexless love. Even Kali you have tried to deform. The naked fierce goddess, who cares two hoots about social propriety! But you prudes have dangled the necklace of severed heads to cover her privates. I will help these gods win freedom from you." She raised the naked dolls above her head.

Satyen called out, "Careful, don't go too far!"
Nisha was glad for the rebuttal, "Like I care about your sentiments! Come, rescue them!" She called the men making clucking sounds with her tongue as though she was calling chickens. Then she lowered her arms, "Poor dolls, why should I destroy them? Just some harmless earthenware - with not even manhood, leave alone divine-hood. Come to think of it; I believe the people around here have also lost their manhood. Shall we test? OK, here I go." She raised her kameez and threw it over her head. The men bowed their heads and stared at the floor.

Paul heard Satyen beside him whisper, "Only one man can save her."

Paul replied, also under his breath, "Yes, but I think he has taken off. I did not see him after dinner."

"Not him, I mean you. Only you can save the day."

"Why me?"

"Don't question, act now."

Paul was pushed forward by those words. He picked the kameez from the ground and stopped Nisha's hands as they were struggling with the buttons on her back. "Raise your arms," he commanded. Her dilated red eyes flared at him. He repeated, gently this time, "Raise your arms. Please Nisha, listen to me." She did. And he slipped the kameez back in place. Then he held her in his embrace, pinning her hands back with his. She fell limp against him and started weeping. The sobs were loud at first. Slowly she quietened and let the tears fall. It was a strange sight. An embracing couple in the meditation hall. The brothers stood around like pillars. Then one by one they left the room.

Paul relaxed his grip on her hands and she struggled no more. His shirt front was getting drenched by her tears. His hand was patting the back of her head, "It's alright, it's alright. This too will pass." She trembled in his arms as spasms caught and left her. Then she let him go slowly and covered her face in her hands.

"Let me drop you home," he said.

She nodded and picked her way over the debris on the floor.

At the threshold they met one of the junior ashram members. He had a bucket with a mop in it and a broom. He looked at her timidly, "Satyen-da says if you clean the hall before tomorrow's morning prayer nobody in the village would know what happened."

There was a catch in Nisha's throat. She asked the boy, "You mean none of you will tell?"

He nodded.

She seized the broom and the bucket and turned around scanning the damage she had done. "Paul, thank you for all your help. Now I will not hold you up."

Paul left.

Satyen was standing in the shadows of the corridor. As Paul passed by he whispered, "Be with her tonight."

Paul's head was just clearing and he wondered what he had been doing in there embracing a lady in that sacred place in front of the brothers.

"*You* be with her tonight," he replied.

Satyen sighed, "I cannot."

"Why?" he challenged, "Cannot be caught passing a night with a woman?"

"I don't care about slander. It's that she is in a delicate state. She is angry with Hiren, and we are all copies of him. Except you. Don't spoil her chance of wiping out some bad deed she incurred today."

"Oh bother," grumbled Paul.

"Take your pillow and blanket. You can sleep in there. Just be a little vigilant."

Nisha was raising up a dust storm. Her eyes were watering. From the dust or were they tears? Paul announced himself, "Hello, I am back," hoping she would not ask why he was back. She raised her head momentarily then continued her chore. He lay down in a corner she had cleaned and watched her move around. Then he caught her leaving the room. He asked, "Where are you going?"
"Don't worry, just to the water cooler."

Paul woke up from a nudge. Nisha was sitting beside him. "Sorry to wake you up, but do you have some needle and thread? This dress is torn." She held up the Radha doll and showed the clothes that needed to be pleated back in place. Paul got the necessaries from his room. As she sat sewing he looked around in surprise, "I must say you have done a good job."
"Yes, five hours of labor to undo five minutes of madness. But how could I help it? I simply lost my mind when I saw it."
"Saw what?"

"When Hiren went for dinner I entered his room. Just to see it for the last time - where he sat advising me on so many things. I felt curious to see it from his perspective and so I walked around to his side of the table. I found a drawer. Opened it. You know, how curiosity works. I would have shut it immediately had I not read my name. It was on a folder. I opened it. It had notes about me: when I came to him, what I asked him, how I was progressing. Even a doctor would not write such details about a patient. What he suggested I do. He writes that sometimes he did not speak, he simply planted thoughts in my mind. I recalled getting some of those thoughts. There were other folders below mine, each with a name on top. Do you see what I saw? I was just a folder for him. And he was my hero, the prince of my dreams. That's all I am. A folder with my psychological records. You must be a folder too. We are just guinea pigs here. This is a laboratory to study human behavior. They control our thoughts. And they use these gods as mascots to fool us. And we think they are a spiritual organization!"

"Nisha, why are so angry that Hiren suggested ideas to you? They were for your own good, weren't they? Tell me something: are you under the impression that you decide your own actions?"

"Of course, I came here of my own free will and I can leave whenever I like. Nobody is paying me; nobody is waiting for my story."

"I thought you *wanted* to help these people, *wanted* to get recognition for it, *wanted* people to read your book, to interview you, invite you for lecture tours. All these brought you here and are keeping you trapped here."

"If my desires are driving me, why should I stay *here*? There are people elsewhere who need help too."

"Something you and I are unaware of brought you here. Call it destiny if you wish, or your inner guide."

"I know why destiny brought me here. There is corruption festering in this ashram. It wants me to expose it."

"Nisha, these people here are very smart. If that was the reason you came here they would know it instantly and show you the door. But, no, they care for you. Satyen sent me to take care of you."

"You are so naïve! Satyen sent you to spy on me. So that I don't uncover any other sinister secret. But now their game is over. And my task here is done. I got my story. Not exactly the one I started with, but a good one nonetheless."

"Nisha, think a little. They are giving you a chance allowing you to clean this mess up."

"Chance? I don't think so. They don't want people to know why it was messed up. They threw a karma spin and I bit the bait."

"Then why did you clean it up?" Paul checked himself just on time. He was going to suggest she could desecrate it again and keep it on display.

Nisha replied, "I cleaned it because of the space. This meditation hall is sacred to many innocent people, even if the guardians are not so innocent. A collective aspiration has created it and they shall maintain it in the future. That is, after these people go, for go they must."

She placed Radha and Krishna beside each other and bowed before them. Then she strode out confidently.

Chapter Sixteen

The fury

They came armed with sticks and stones. Twenty or thirty of them. Some tribal people, some townsfolk. Nisha at their head. "Open the doors!" they screamed, "We have a search warrant."

The brothers were swiftly assembling in the courtyard.

"Can we talk?" asked Satyen.

"We want action," yelled the people.

"Do you need weapons to search an ashram? Don't you trust your hands and eyes?"

Nisha answered, "We don't trust *you*. Tell us, who is sponsoring this research?"

"This is not a research center," answered Satyen.

"OK, let me put it bluntly. Who is paying for your food?"

"We do it ourselves, from our services as teachers and healers, we get royalty from books, we conduct study camps, we go on lecture tours."

"What is this foreigner doing here?" Nisha pointed her finger at Paul.

Paul winced, "*foreigner*", is that all he was for her? Not even a name?

"He can answer for himself." Satyen looked at Paul.

"I am here to educate myself," answered Paul.

"About what?" asked Nisha glaring at him.

"About mystic India."

"That's a cover. He is a CIA agent. America is sponsoring this center."

Chapter 16

Paul answered, "I just hope you are not so loose with your facts when you write journalistic reports."

"Loose?" Nisha was furious, she turned to her men, "This psychology lab is breeding mind readers. And they use us as experimental rats. They control us with their minds. Then these people will be imported to America and get into espionage. They will tease out strategies from the enemy camp. They will report on policies that may harm America's foreign interests. They will catch criminals while they are plotting their crimes."

"She *is* creative!" exclaimed Paul.

"Not really," answered Satyen. "She has read. During the cold war the CIA recruited such people. It was before your time, so maybe you don't know."

"See," Nisha pointed her finger at Satyen. "He confesses."

"Now she has lost her rational faculty," sighed a brother.

"Oh no," she turned upon him, "Ask the American. He wanted to take Hiren to America."

Satyen replied jovially, "Sounds like a good national policy - stem crime before it is committed."

"Crime for one man is a good deed for another. *Terrorism* for some is *revolution* for others. Who are you to judge what good social policy is? You are not men of the world. Do you have a mission statement for this organization?"

"Woman, call it an ashram!" cried Paul, gloating in his revenge. If he was no more than a *foreigner*, she would be *woman* to him.

"It's alright, Paul," said Satyen. He addressed the rabble, "We have no written mission statement because it is a simple one - just a single word – yoga."

Nisha shouted, "Yet another cover. Comrades, are you ready?" She turned towards her accomplices. A chorus of "Yes!" went up. They stopped abruptly. Satyen had raised his hand. He said slowly, chewing every word, "There is a good destruction and a bad one, just as there is a good creation and a bad one. Discriminate properly - if you must act."
Still with her back to Satyen Nisha said, "Don't get fooled by this man's words. He is hypnotizing us. Come on, let's go."

As the men began to run Satyen held Nisha back by her arm. She looked at his hand touching her arm and smirked. The men surged past them.
"Will you take a last suggestion from me?" he asked.
She stared at him angrily.
"You may not want people to look at your private file."
He let her go.

She rushed to Hiren's room. People were already turning things upside down. She made for the drawer and rescued her file. Then she slipped out and quietly went up to the terrace. Leaning from this vantage point she inspected the chaos below. Chairs and desks were tumbling out into the open. Sticks could be heard striking the ground. Once in a while a voice was raised in rude questioning, "Show us the secret hiding place! Where do you keep your money? Is that all? What else are you hiding? We are warning you. The sanctum will be raided."

The brothers were huddled in the courtyard answering in inaudible voices. Satyen was a pillar of calm, though some others looked distressed. Paul was the only one jumping about, trying to stop the sticks from falling on delicate objects such as the water cooler, the ceiling fans, the kitchenware.

Nisha sat down leaning against the parapet of the terrace and opened her file. She had read the first few pages before. Now she turned to a new page. Hiren's handwriting read, "Paul met Nisha for the first time. An interesting phenomenon occurred. Paul saw her wearing exaggerated ornaments, aboriginal ones, such as earrings that made her earlobes sore, necklace of some rough material choking her neck, hairpins hooked right into the thin flesh of her skull. Paul was fascinated by her tolerance. He asked why she had such a grotesque getup."

Nisha was confused. She never wore ornaments, not even small ones, and these outlandish ones were … yes, grotesque. She must have looked ugly to Paul. Suddenly she remembered how Paul was staring at her. Hiren noted that Paul saw her true image because he was free of all prejudices about her. He saw with his intuition, not with the mind's eyes. He was seeing her subtle form.

Hiren wrote, "She describes herself as writer, activist, journalist, deliverer of the weak. She is proud of a father who was in the Air Force, proud of her elite school, proud of her English accent. Even proud that she has my attention. Now she has to live up to these definitions of herself. She is hurting herself in the process but does not realize it." She remembered Hiren had told her to let go of her burden. Only then could she discover her true self. She wondered, was writing her calling? Was activism her calling? Or did they matter only to her fabricated self?

Then came a section where Hiren wrote like a doctor. "The disease has aggravated. She has become a poor listener." What disease? She was healthy. Soon she found a clue – "Frustration upon frustration has made her a closed person. I am unable to cure. The only thing I can do is offer her problem to the divine."

Was she really so frustrated? No, it could not be. Hiren had special insight. Yes, her work with the tribal people was leading nowhere. She had come to write a story where she would be the savior queen. But the fight never seemed to end. Hiren had warned her often not to look for an ending. "Life is an unending journey. It does not need to have a neat ending like a story. You are seeking something you may not find."

"On another front too she has hit a wall," wrote Hiren, "The love inside her wants to express itself. The tribal are too simple for her, and we in the ashram are not cut out for a romantic life. She does not want to mingle with the townsfolk. She will again be frustrated unless she realizes her life has another purpose." Her frustrations started nauseating her. From down below the sporadic sounds of breaking objects crashed into her silent retreat.

Towards the end Hiren wrote, "Meeting me is harming her now. I must conclude this project, and sad to say it will be abrupt. But I don't see any other way. Her worship of Humanism has left her a rebel." Hiren's voice floated in her mind. "You become like the object you worship. Be careful what you worship." She had welcomed his comment because she knew whom she worshipped – him. Surely he was worthy of her worship. But now she understood what he meant. She had banished the gods and seated humanity in that spot. And not a brilliant humankind – a downtrodden, lost, prejudiced lot. The journal went on, "The simple trust of the unlettered folk have given her a false sense of power. There is a danger she will use it. If not to create, then to destroy. Power cannot sit idle. One needs to be very pure not to misuse it. We do not know if destruction is needed for some future creation. But only the strong can clear the ground for a new manifestation. An uncontrolled fury turns upon its source."

The journal ended there. Nisha got up and looked over the parapet. A chaotic scene met her eyes - a pile of desks with their drawers opened, shattered pieces of earthenware, utensils, lentils and pulses scattered all over, jute bags ripped opened and rice grains dribbling out. She screamed, "Stop! Everybody stop! Enough!"

Her team members came out of the rooms and looked up at her. One commented, "We have found no documents or computers or even cell phones. This is a medieval place. They still use earthen jugs."

"Alright, now arrange everything back," she ordered.

"Eh? What did you say?" they asked her.

"You heard me. Do it!" she was grinding her teeth in rage.

"And who are you to order us around? *You* do it."

"Pick those lentils, grain by grain. Pick those utensils and put them back where you found them," she gesticulated furiously.

"Just because you are standing on a high perch does not make you a queen. You have wasted enough of our time already." The rabble was heating up.

"And humiliated us."

"We have accused these poor sadhus mistakenly."

"Who will suffer its consequences?"

"Not us. She did it. She instigated us. We are innocent, we just obeyed her hunch.

Get her down, the witch!"

Some men started climbing the stairs to reach the terrace. Satyen's loud voice arrested them, "Men, show some decency in the house of the lord. Run along, we don't need your help to clean up."

Then men picked their sticks and left grumbling and swearing.

Nisha was crying as she walked down and came up to Satyen. She asked him in a shaking voice, "Why did he treat me so? Was I nothing more than a folder?"

Satyen answered without rancor in his voice, "Child, *you* were not a folder. Your progress was written down in a folder. You will allow people to have personal journals I hope? That was Hiren's way of organizing his thoughts. A folder for each person he helped."

"It hurts to think that he had already foreseen an end."

"Nisha, do you think you will forever be the person you are now? You will write new chapters in your life. You will create new folders for yourself. When we meet a new person, we open a folder. When that person drifts away we close it. It happens without our conscious effort. Every encounter in our life is a folder. When children leave home parents close their folders. When you left home you closed your parent's folder. Your school life was a project. Your work life is a project. Within that your helping the tribal is a project. Within that every petition you make is a project. This very life is a project in your soul's adventure. It will close when you die. Then another folder will be opened with another name on the cover. This ashram is a project. On this same spot there may have been a kingdom in the last century. And a lake in the previous. This earth is a project of the creator. This universe itself may be an experiment. It may end in the waste bin of time. Or it may last forever. Maybe the creator himself is a project. An experiment by the Unknown. What do we know? How much do we count? And you have the foolhardiness to ask why you are a folder? Many will die with no one having written a word in their folder. And you had a person like Hiren filling up pages for you. Many in your place would feel immensely lucky. Use that folder as your guidebook for the rest of your life."

Nisha's knelt down by Satyen's feet and sobbed. The brothers were dispersing. They had many things to do. Satyen walked away from her and entered the meditation hall. Paul followed him, sweating from his efforts, ready to do whatever he would be asked to do. He was taken by surprise. Satyen was lying prostrate before the image of Kali his palms joined together in supplication.

Chapter Seventeen

Love

The dust had not yet settled the next morning. They were exhausted and had all gone to sleep late the previous night. Paul got up hearing his cell phone buzz. There was a text message from Nisha, "Urgent, please meet me." For all practical purposes he had written her off as crazy, so he quietly ignored her. Half way through the day he had a terrible presentiment. What if she was about to do something insane, like take her own life, and he was the last straw? He hurried to her hotel expecting her to have checked out. But she was there locked up in her room, apparently crying. When she saw Paul she got up and handed him a thick envelope for Satyen, "Can you deliver this for me please?"

"Why don't you yourself?"

"I couldn't face them. Please, I beg of you," she mumbled and locked the door abruptly, cutting him out.

Paul handed the envelope to Satyen. He opened it and out came some cash. Satyen counted it, "This should cover *our* damages. But I don't know how she is going to repair the damage she did to herself and the others she brought with her."

"So are you going to let her go? It would be in your rights to put her behind bars."

"I need not worry about that. Hasn't she done it herself?"

A few days later Satyen found Paul and asked him to call on Nisha. He wanted to speak with her. Paul obeyed though he did not expect to find her in town. Ever since Hiren's departure the ashram was as though in mourning. The pole practice was lifeless. The dining room was as silent as the meditation hall. It seemed the brothers were introspecting. Paul expected every day fresh announcements of people wishing to leave. Satyen himself was out on some lecture tour for a few days after the incident. Maybe he had timed it that way. Without Hiren the ashram was a different place. So Paul welcomed his new assignment and slipped out.

The hotel manager said Nisha was around. Paul knocked on her door and announced himself, "Care for some tea?"
She opened the door and nodded him in. She shook her head dejectedly. "I don't deserve."
"Oh, don't you get there. Of course you don't deserve. So what? Wash your face and comb your hair. Not those sandals, wear the shoes. Show me some of the flora and fauna out here. I am craving for a walk."

They walked in silence till they were out of town. This side thinned out into a marshland. Tall fennel groves made the air fragrant with their sweetness. Nisha collected a few seeds and shared them with Paul. After nibbling on them Paul exclaimed, "Oh, no, we should have waited for tea. Now the tea will taste weird."
"Oh tea, I almost forgot," trailed off Nisha.
"I was hoping you know some place around here."

"Yes, I know a good place. It's roadside food though. Can you risk it?"

"Sure, boiled water is pure."

"I was thinking of some snacks too. Come to think of it, I am famished," Nisha sounded like her old self. Paul felt relieved. She turned around, "We need to go back to town though."

Hot masala tea in earthen pots that singed your fingertips if you did not dance it from one hand to another - that is what Paul had. Nisha ate a good helping of kachauri with potato curry. Her spirits were getting restored with every morsel. "You don't know what you are missing," she kept saying between greedy bites.

And then she became morose again. They walked in silence for a while. Paul did not know how he could break this tone deaf silence. Then the last house ended and they were in the marshland. Far away a line of trees defined the forest. Nisha walked faster as though she was reaching her friend's house and was eager to meet her. Pointing at a bush a few paces away she said, "Do you see those red flowers on the bush?"

"Yes, pretty."

"Now I will perform a magic. Watch carefully."

She ran towards the bush and clapped her hands. There was a fluttering of wings and all the red flowers flew away. They were a colony of red breasted birds. Paul applauded and caught up with her.

She pranced forward like a child, pointing out this bird and that. The heron on one leg was meditating on a fish. Some smaller birds with pointed beaks were poking insects out of the mud in jerky movements. They flew past the hermit heron, who held his marble poise. A flock of even smaller birds rushed in from somewhere and landed on the water. Then restless for more adventure rose up in a crowd and toured the swamps again. The heron plunged its beak in the water. A family of ducks swam around the pool. Everything was in harmony.

"Imagine a mine here with its noisy polluting engines caving in this place. It would destroy this watershed. Migratory birds love this place. Some of them come from the North Pole. In your country this would be declared a natural reserve. Here we are fighting to preserve even human habitat. And it is a thankless battle. Worse still now perhaps they will not trust me anymore."
Paul ignored the last comment, "The mines are not here, so you have been successful so far. Don't give up yet."
"All I am doing is buying time. The clock is ticking."

They walked in silence watching the red breasted birds that had returned to the bushes. They sat like cherries on a cake. Paul started singing the nursery rhyme, "Sing a song of six pence…" Nisha joined in.
"Wow, you have a melodious voice!" he exclaimed.
"Oh, I haven't sung forever."
"Sing something."

Paul waited for a long time. Slowly Nisha started humming and then came the words. The song wasn't in English, but he knew it must have been an emotional one. Once or twice she choked and trailed off. He was patient and did not ask what it meant or why she choked. She completed the song and said, "It feels good now. Something inside was knotted up."

"Someday you will tell me what it means?" he asked gently.

She nodded. "You know the other day you asked what was I pre-occupied with. And I said it was the book I was writing about these tribal people. In reality it was this: in my mind I was fantasizing what I would answer to the interviewer. Imagine, the book isn't written, and I am already famous! Even if the book gets written, what are the chances it will become well known? I am just one in a million writers. But that is what I was doing to myself. And I dropped the pail of milk."

"You have not dropped it yet. You can still write a book that will make you famous!"

"Don't. I am not in any fantasy world anymore. I thought I was so great Hiren would fall for me."

"You loved him a lot?"

"I have been unlucky in love. I mean, it's not that boys and men did not get attached to me, or I to them. But after two years, I got bored. I saw too many flaws in them and I started hating them. I ran. There was a period of relief, then again the old refrain caught on. I wanted to express love but could not find a man worthy enough. And then I met Hiren. He was a hero in all ways. But he treated me in a distant fashion. I dropped umpteen hints. He waved them away."

"He has devoted his life for something other than worldly pursuits."

"I know that. I did not want us to be entangled in any melodramatic romance. I had had enough of that. Nature has given us this drive, why not use it? I did not want it to be a physical relationship. I wanted to work out something else, something pure, elevating even. I wanted us to realize some sort of union of the soul. And now he is gone. I feel so empty, as though this whole universe is laughing at my stupid hopes."

Paul put his arm around her and drew her close. You are intelligent, skillful, smart and passionate about life. Don't give up. You will find someone willing and somewhat heroic too. Only don't go about comparing him to Hiren."

She nodded sadly. They walked close together holding hands. She felt healed. He felt fulfilled. Then he saw the birds with pointy beaks stabbing at the mud and suddenly started laughing, "I wonder how those birds kiss!"

She stopped to look at him, a curious smile on her face. He blushed, "I don't know why…" He stopped. She was also saying something. They both stopped talking. After a pause when they spoke, it was at the same time again. She started giggling and he was relieved his comment was not taken badly.

"You first," he bowed.

"No, you," she laughed.

"I was saying..." began Paul and then stopped, "If you laugh so loudly how can you hear me? Ok, here I go again. I was saying – I don't know why I made that silly remark."

She said, "And I was going to say – you stole the very words out of my mouth!"

"Now you are just making fun of me," he complained.

"No, really. But I am confused. Was it *your* thought I stole or was it *my* thought you stole?"

"You influenced me, I am innocent," he played along.

"Innocent? Not anymore!"

She rose on her toes and kissed him quickly on the lips. "Now, what do you say?"

He held her face and kissed her again, slowly this time, enjoying the taste of her laughter.

"Twice guilty," he bowed.

"Two is a bad number," she chirped.

"Is that so? Who am I to argue?"

They kissed again.

Suddenly Nisha looked up and saw the ashram. She said a hasty goodbye and was about to go when they heard Satyen greet her. Paul waved to Satyen, feeling like a hero having brought the culprit to the court. The three sat on the steps of the veranda facing the garden. Nisha'e eyes filled with tears as she noticed the plants, crushed to death. Satyen asked after her as if nothing had happened: how she was doing with her project, when was her next court appearance, if the hotel room was tolerable, whether she was eating well. He said Madhu had room for a guest and she would be happy to have Nisha. Madhu is a good companion and perhaps the Gita classes would interest

Nisha? Nisha had swallowed her tongue, but her tearful eyes said it all.

Satyen explained, "This thing called romantic love is a complicated business when you are submerged in it. And yes, it is hard to keep afloat. The rational part of the brain gets drowned in some hormonal fluid that inhibits its proper functioning. People become so absorbed in each other they forget to step back. Tell me, both of you, on the way back from the marshes did you notice any birds?" Paul winced, Nisha blushed. They were glad they did not have to answer the question.

"Yet this is one of nature's tricks to keep the species going. Thus it overpowers most people. Once love settles down and our heads emerge from the hormone soup, we see our partner in the light of common day. Some people part. Many others live a compromised existence. There are some rewards – the pleasure of helping others grow, provide security, share moments together, do things that are possible to do only with the other sex. Society has played its role. It has created marriage laws and child support. We are often reminded that we are gregarious creatures, too much solitude will drive us crazy, our body needs affection, our heart needs to give and take, old age is difficult, and so on. It is a commerce of sentiments. And like a good marketer the practical voice wins over the adventurer in us. We grow old. We give in."

"A love that defies time is neither achievable, nor desirable. Remember you become the person you worship. Would you like to become a copy of another human, however great he may be? A person who has his eye on progress will move on. Moving on does not mean jumping from lover to lover, but placing love in the right place. Human love is imperfect because exclusive love for one makes you indifferent to others. If you have a big heart you can expand your love to encompass more people. Not just your family or clan or community or nation. Embrace humanity and all the creatures of this planet, and even the non-living things. See this planet as a living organism; see this creation as a gift from some ultimate Benevolence. When you can love from this vantage point, then you can truly love. And this is the love we in the ashram want to develop. A pure unselfish love for all.

Hiren was such a lover. He loved all in equal measure; and he gave more than anyone could contain. It is because you wanted him exclusively, because your love is human, that you failed to understand him. And since everybody in the ashram is not as pure-hearted as Hiren, and therefore level-headed, we keep them away from women. It is not that women are barred from living in the ashram, it is that men are not strong enough to have them here.

I think you are naturally blessed to practice the yoga of love. You will have to exceed your demand for a personal lover though. I understand it was a long-cherished dream of yours. But you are lucky. Your path is not strewn with flowers to distract you. You do not need a partner to practice this path. The divine is your lover. You don't see him because you look for him in men's hearts. He is indeed in every man and woman, but he is not trapped there alone."

Nisha nodded, "I need to re-arrange my feelings. It is quite a mess inside, so much so that I cannot see the blessings you are talking about." She started sniffing as the tears rolled down her cheeks, "And Paul, thank you for your kindness. It was well-timed."

She wiped her eyes and got up resolutely. She joined her palms in salutation and bowed before Satyen. Then she tuned on her heels and walked out.

Paul looked at her back and whispered, "The activist's march - not looking back, not hesitant, aiming straight for her goal."

"Well, of course," commented Satyen, "Hiren would not waste time on a faint-hearted one. His very absence is going to guide her now."

"But his absence is weighing on me sorely."

"Don't get too used to the prop. It's time to start the hard climb yourself. Some of the brothers are also shaken. Those who will win this battle will remain, and the rest will fall out, which is what we want. This is an arduous journey and it is best for the weak not to attempt the steeper climb. Sometimes those standing on the highest peaks sacrifice to help others progress faster."

Epilogue

"Satyen, give me a something I can take back home."

"Take the word 'Aum'."

"Ah, that intriguing word! You know what I am reminded of when I hear the word Aum before every chant? 'In the beginning was the Word, and the Word was with God, and the Word was God.' Is Aum this word?"

"Yes."

"What does it mean?"

"That is a very difficult question to answer."

"But people will ask me what it means, and then what should I tell me them?"

"Tell them to meditate on it. Some of our own rishis have spent the better part of their lives fathoming this one word."

"Come on, Satyen, you can do better. Give me a little glimpse of it."

"So you want to know what Aum is…let me see… When born, our first cry begins with 'A'. And the last breath we utter ends in 'M'. In between is the wonder and the questioning and the despair and the growing. In between is the stumble and the fall, the walk and the run. The geometry of lines, the geometry of relationships, the geometry of doubt wrinkling the face. And the questioning. Why is this happening to me? Why am I here? And the forgetting. The duties taking over. The schooling, the earning. A pursuit. A love. The inter-braiding with other lives. Disentangling. Re-entangling in other forms.

And the knocking goes on. The knocking of the fledgling's beak against the egg shell. There is something beyond the shell. Even beyond the grand egg shell, the universe. And then the crimes of ambition. The gilded chains, the savior swords. Success with its lizard eyes watching our every move. The knocking resumes, more urgently. Then the respite of forgetting. The gloating in glory, the bloating of the ego. Death of a near one. Moments of clarity. Always a relative clarity. Then return of the cycles.

Suddenly disease - that stark reminder. Breeding helplessness. Bringing humility. If we are lucky. Otherwise bitterness. And again the refrain of questioning. What was the purpose? And *my* purpose? Was there a goal? That I perchance missed? And the despondency that eats at the soul's roots. Have I cheated myself? And the world falls away. Instantly. The groping. The knocking. Is the shell giving way? A parting of clouds. The sun streaming in. And one day the last utterance 'M'. From the first to the last breath all we did was utter a long Aum. All our life is nothing but a single Aum that the mighty Sacrificer offers to the Fire. And while he pours the oblation He chants 'Aum'."

Made in the USA
Charleston, SC
03 August 2015